Copyright © 2025 by Holly Symons
All rights reserved.

No part of this book may be reproduced, scanned, or distributed in any printed or electronic form without permission.
This book is a work of fiction. Names, characters, places, and incidents are either the product of the author's imagination or used fictitiously.
Hardback - ISBN: 978-1-923567-36-8
Paperback - ISBN: 978-1-923567-37-5
eBook - ISBN: 978-1-923567-38-2

Cover design by **Holly Symons**
First Edition

For More, Please Visit
HollySymons.com.au

"Your shine isn't the problem; their muddy hands are."

Protect.

Peace.

Repeat.

The Crumb Queens:

A Girlfriend's Guide on How to Spot, Stop, and Survive Fake Friends, Family Foes, and the Lonely in Between

First Addition

~

HOLLY SYMONS

This book is intended for educational and self-help purposes only. It is not a substitute for professional therapy, counselling, or medical advice. If you are struggling with your mental health, please seek support from a qualified professional.

Author's Note
(Trigger Warning + Support)

This book talks honestly about toxic relationships, family dynamics, and emotional struggles. Some chapters may bring up strong or unexpected feelings. If at any point you feel overwhelmed, please pause, take a breath, and reach out for support - you do not have to go through it alone.

Free, confidential help is available:

- **AUSTRALIA: Lifeline – Call 13 11 14 or text 0477 13 11 14**
- **NEW ZEALAND: 1737 Need to talk? Call or text 1737**
- **UK & IRELAND: Samaritans – Call 116 123 (freephone)**
- **USA & CANADA: 988 Suicide & Crisis Lifeline – Call or text 988**

TABLE OF CONTENTS

AUTHOR'S NOTE (TRIGGER WARNING + SUPPORT)	7

ACT 1 – THE FRIEND ZONE FROM HELL   1

CHAPTER 1: THE SWEET TALKERS WHO ROT YOUR TEETH	2
CHAPTER 2: WHEN "LET'S CATCH UP" MEANS "I NEED SOMETHING"	7
CHAPTER 3: THE SELFIE FRIEND WHO ONLY CALLS IN GOOD LIGHTING	12
CHAPTER 4: HOW TO SPOT A COMPLIMENT WRAPPED IN A JAB	17
CHAPTER 5: THE BORROWER WHO FORGETS WHAT THEY BORROWED	22
CHAPTER 6: GROUP CHATS THAT FEEL LIKE HUNGER GAMES	27
CHAPTER 7: THE FRIEND WHO LOVES YOU, UNTIL YOU'RE DOING BETTER THAN THEM	32
CHAPTER 8: WHEN EVERY STORY YOU TELL BECOMES ABOUT THEM	37
CHAPTER 9: THE FLAKY FRIEND OLYMPICS: GOLD MEDAL GHOSTING	42
CHAPTER 10: HOW TO AVOID BECOMING THE FREE THERAPIST	46
CHAPTER 11: YOUR SECRETS ARE NOT GROUP CURRENCY	50
CHAPTER 12: HOW TO SURVIVE FRIENDS WHO "FORGET" TO INVITE YOU	55
CHAPTER 13: FRENEMIES AND THEIR SLOW DRIP SABOTAGE	59
CHAPTER 14: SOCIAL MEDIA STALKERS DISGUISED AS FRIENDS	64

- **Chapter 15: How to Exit a Friendship Without Setting Yourself on Fire** — 68
- **Chapter 16: The Energy Vampire Detox Plan** — 73
- **Chapter 17: Boundary Bootcamp for People Who Hate Confrontation** — 78
- **# Bonus Chapter: The Misunderstood People Pleaser** — 82
- **Chapter 18: When Your "Bestie" Is the First to Doubt You** — 87
- **Chapter 19: How to Recognise Love Bombing in Friendships** — 92
- **Chapter 20: The "One-Up" Friend Who Always Has It Worse or Better** — 97
- **Chapter 21: When They Copy Everything but Your Struggles** — 101
- **Chapter 22: The Coward's Apology and Why It Doesn't Count** — 106
- **Chapter 23: How to Stop Being Everyone's Emotional Dump Bin** — 111
- **Chapter 24: The Friend Who Shows Up Only for the Fun Stuff** — 115
- **Chapter 25: Why "No" Is the New Self-Care** — 119
- **Chapter 26: The Secret Test of True Friendship** — 123
- **Chapter 27: How to Spot Jealousy in a Smile** — 127
- **Chapter 28: The Friend Who Turns Into a Stranger Overnight** — 131
- **Chapter 29: Emotional Hoarders: They Take, Never Give** — 136
- **Chapter 30: What to Do When They Choose Sides Against You** — 140
- **Chapter 31: Friend Breakups Hurt Worse Than Boyfriend Breakups (and How to Heal)** — 145
- **Chapter 32: The Long Game of Letting Go** — 149
- **Chapter 33: Your Next Best Friend Might Be You** — 153

ACT 2 – THE FAMILY CIRCUS 157

Chapter 34: When Family Feels Like a Full-Time Job You Didn't Apply For 158
Chapter 35: The Difference Between Boundaries and Betrayal 162
Chapter 36: Why "That's Just How They Are" Is Gaslighting in Disguise 166
Chapter 37: The Family Member Who Always Keeps Score 170
Chapter 38: How to Stop Explaining Yourself to People Who Don't Listen 174
Chapter 39: When Your Achievements Are Met with Silence 178
Chapter 40: The Relative Who Needs You but Can't Stand You 181
Chapter 41: Holidays Without the Drama (Yes, It's Possible) 184
Chapter 42: The Gossip Mill That Runs on Your Business 187
Chapter 43: Being the Truth Teller in a Family That Loves Lies 191
Chapter 44: How to Survive the Golden Child Syndrome (When You're Not It) 195
Chapter 45: The Art of the Strategic Disinvite 199
Chapter 46: The Emotional Cost of the "Peacemaker" Role 203
Chapter 47: Why Going No Contact Is Sometimes the Healthiest Move 207
Chapter 48: How to Set Boundaries with Parents Without Feeling Like a Monster 211
Chapter 49: The Auntie Who Turns Every Conversation into a Roast 215
Chapter 50: When Siblings Become Strangers 219

CHAPTER 51: HOW TO HANDLE IN-LAWS WITHOUT LOSING YOUR SANITY 224
CHAPTER 52: WHY FAMILY GROUP CHATS ARE EMOTIONAL MINEFIELDS 229
CHAPTER 53: THE UNCLE WHO DRINKS AND THINKS HE'S WISE 234
CHAPTER 54: NAVIGATING FUNERALS WITHOUT DIGGING EMOTIONAL GRAVES 238
CHAPTER 55: THE COUSIN WHO COMPETES LIKE IT'S THE OLYMPICS 243
CHAPTER 56: HOW TO SPOT FINANCIAL MANIPULATION IN FAMILY 247
CHAPTER 57: BREAKING THE CYCLE OF FAMILY GUILT TRIPS 251
CHAPTER 58: WHY YOU'RE NOT OBLIGATED TO PLAY HOST FOR TOXIC PEOPLE 255
CHAPTER 59: THE MYTH OF "BLOOD IS THICKER THAN WATER" 259
CHAPTER 60: HOW TO BUILD YOUR OWN CHOSEN FAMILY 263

ACT 3 – THE RISE 267

CHAPTER 61: HOW TO REBUILD WHEN YOU'RE STARTING FROM ZERO 268
CHAPTER 62: STOP EXPLAINING AND START LIVING 271
CHAPTER 63: FINDING YOUR PEOPLE IN THE WILD 274
CHAPTER 64: THE 90-DAY BOUNDARY RESET 277
CHAPTER 65: RELEARNING TRUST WITHOUT LOSING YOUR GUARD 280
CHAPTER 66: WHY SELF-RESPECT FEELS LONELY AT FIRST 284
CHAPTER 67: SAYING "NO" WITHOUT THE GUILT HANGOVER 287

CHAPTER 68: HOW TO KEEP YOUR PEACE WHEN THEY PUSH BACK — 290

CHAPTER 69: TURNING OLD WOUNDS INTO WISDOM — 294

CHAPTER 70: THE ART OF THE SOFT EXIT FROM TOXIC SPACES — 298

CHAPTER 71: HOW TO LOVE WITHOUT LOSING YOURSELF AGAIN — 301

CHAPTER 72: BECOMING THE MAIN CHARACTER OF YOUR OWN LIFE — 304

CHAPTER 73: WHY SELF-CARE ISN'T ALWAYS PRETTY — 307

CHAPTER 74: THE POWER OF GOING QUIET BEFORE YOU GO LOUD — 310

CHAPTER 75: HOW TO KEEP SMALL WINS FROM FEELING SMALL — 313

CHAPTER 76: THE BEAUTY OF HAVING FEWER, DEEPER CONNECTIONS — 317

CHAPTER 77: WHY VALIDATION IS AN INSIDE JOB — 320

CHAPTER 78: LEARNING TO CELEBRATE YOURSELF OUT LOUD — 323

CHAPTER 79: BECOMING UNSHAKEABLE WITHOUT BECOMING UNFEELING — 326

CHAPTER 80: HOW TO HANDLE PEOPLE WHO HATE YOUR BOUNDARIES — 329

CHAPTER 81: WHEN TO WALK AWAY BEFORE YOU BURN OUT — 333

CHAPTER 82: BUILDING EMOTIONAL MUSCLE FOR THE LONG GAME — 337

CHAPTER 83: HOW TO SPOT REAL LOVE AND REAL FRIENDSHIP EARLY ON — 341

CHAPTER 84: THE SELF-RESPECT CHECKLIST — 345

ACT 4 – THE QUIET AFTER THE STORM — 349

- Chapter 85: Why Loneliness Isn't a Sign You've Done Something Wrong — 350
- Chapter 86: How to Stop Romanticising the People You Walked Away From — 354
- Chapter 87: The Difference Between Being Alone and Being Lonely — 358
- Chapter 88: How to Fill Your Own Cup (Without Waiting for Someone Else to Pour) — 361
- Chapter 89: Relearning Fun Without an Audience — 364
- Chapter 90: Finding Peace in Your Own Company — 367
- Chapter 91: The Joy of Saying "No Plans" and Meaning It — 370
- Chapter 92: Why Some Days Will Still Hurt (And That's Okay) — 373
- Chapter 93: Making Your Home Your Safe Space — 376
- Chapter 94: The Beauty of Small, Consistent Routines — 378
- Chapter 95: How to Date Yourself Without Feeling Silly — 381
- Chapter 96: Finding New Hobbies Without the Friend Drama — 384
- Chapter 97: How to Make Peace with "It Ended" — 387
- Chapter 98: Choosing the Right People to Let Back In — 390
- Chapter 99: The Science of Building New Neural Pathways for Joy — 393
- Chapter 100: When Loneliness Turns into Freedom — 397
- Chapter 101: The First Laugh After the Storm — 400
- Chapter 102: Why "Better Alone" Can Be Better Forever — 403

Chapter 103: How to Spot When You're Ready to Connect Again   406
Chapter 104: The New Life You Build Is the Real Revenge   409

ACT 1 – The Friend Zone from Hell

How to spot, stop, and survive fake friends without losing your sparkle.

Chapter 1:
The Sweet Talkers
Who Rot Your Teeth

(Because cavities aren't just for sugar lovers.)

There's a special kind of fake friend who doesn't show up in your life wearing a "Warning: I Will Ruin You" T-shirt. No. They arrive coated in sugar, speaking in soft, syrupy tones that make you feel like the most special person in the room. They'll tell you you're gorgeous, inspiring, talented, and "literally my favourite human." You'll think you've found your hype squad, your soul sister, your brunch-and-bubble buddy for life.

And then, little by little, you'll realise they're not sugar — they're high-fructose toxic syrup.

Sweet talkers are experts in *verbal seduction*. They know how to make you feel safe, so you'll open the vault and hand them the keys to your trust. They sprinkle compliments like confetti, but each one is coated with a subtle aftertaste you can't quite place at first – until one day you realise your sparkle's dulled, your energy's low, and your confidence has been quietly hollowed out like a chocolate bunny after Easter.

The Tell-Tale Signs You've Got a Sweet Talker

1. **They Love You Loudly... in Public.**

   In front of people, they're your biggest fan. They'll gush about you like you just discovered penicillin. But behind closed doors? They might "jokingly" point out your flaws, belittle your wins, or dismiss your dreams as "cute."

2. **They Mirror You Like a Funhouse Reflection.**

   Ever notice how their opinions, style, and even slang morph into yours? Imitation may be the sincerest form of flattery, but with them, it's flattery with a side of identity theft.

3. **Every Compliment Has a Cavity.**

   "You're so brave for wearing that colour." Translation: "I'd never wear that colour because I have taste, but you do you."

4. **They Weaponise Gratitude.**

   They'll gush about how much they "owe you" — until you actually need something. Then suddenly their calendar is more jammed than a Christmas fruitcake.

Why They Do It

Sweet talkers don't always start out with malicious intent. Some are insecure and use charm to keep people close because they fear abandonment. Others use flattery as a calculated strategy, a way to gain influence, information, or access. Either way, their charm is a mask, and it's exhausting to keep up with someone whose "niceness" comes with fine print.

How to Stop Them From Rottin' Your Shine

1. **Don't Confuse Compliments with Character.**

Praise means nothing if their actions don't match their words. Watch what they *do*, not what they *say*.

2. **Run Every Compliment Through a Truth Filter.**

   Ask yourself: "Is this meant to lift me up… or position them above me?"

3. **Limit Emotional Access.**

   Sweet talkers thrive when you give them your secrets, plans, and dreams. Keep your inner circle small and your personal life locked tighter than your Wi-Fi password.

4. **Test for Reciprocity.**

   Try this: stop initiating contact for two weeks. See if they reach out when you're not actively feeding them attention. If not, you have your answer.

Surviving Without Losing Your Sparkle

The goal isn't to become a cynical hermit who trusts no one. The goal is to be discerning. You can accept kindness without swallowing the hook. You can enjoy sugar without living in a dental emergency.

Because at the end of the day, sweet talkers aren't bad because they're nice. They're bad because their "nice" is a marketing campaign, and you're not buying.

You've got better things to do than audition for a friendship that was never real.

And remember, darling:

You are the candy. They are just the wrapper.

Chapter 2:
When "Let's Catch Up" Means "I Need Something"

(Spoiler: it's not your company they're craving.)

We've all had *that* message pop up.

"Hey stranger! Let's catch up soon!"

And for a split second, your heart leaps. Maybe they miss you. Maybe they've been thinking of you. Maybe they finally realised you're the Beyoncé of their social circle and they're ready to make amends.

Then… ten minutes into "catching up," they drop it:

They need a favour. Money. Your Netflix password. Someone to help them move *again*. Or worse, they're trying to sell you an "amazing business opportunity" that suspiciously looks like a pyramid with better lighting.

The Catch-Up Con

This is the emotional equivalent of putting "free samples" on a sign and then charging $5 for the toothpick.

They lure you in with the promise of genuine connection, then blindside you with the invoice, an invoice that's always payable in your time, energy, or resources.

Red Flags That This 'Catch-Up' Is Really a Catch

1. **The Sudden Reunion After Months of Silence**

    If they haven't messaged you since the last time they needed something, congratulations, you're not a friend, you're a vending machine.

2. **The "Warm-Up Questions" Are Rushed**

    They ask how you are, but it's like watching someone fast-forward a movie to get to their favourite part. "Uh-huh… uh-huh… anyway…"

3. **They Casually Drop Their Problem Like It's Your Job**

    It starts small: "I've just been sooo stressed lately." Then, like a plot twist you saw coming, you're suddenly being volunteered as the solution.

4. **You Leave the Conversation Feeling Drained, Not Filled**

    Real catch-ups leave you feeling closer. Catch-up cons leave you feeling like you should send them an invoice.

Why They Do It

People who use "catching up" as a smokescreen often *do* know they're being transactional — but they think disguising it in friendliness makes it okay. For others, it's unconscious: they see you as capable, dependable, and available. Which sounds flattering, until you realise they only value you for what you can provide.

How to Spot the Motive Early

- **Ask Questions Back** — If you get vague answers or they dodge talking about themselves, they're steering toward their real agenda.
- **Delay the Favour** — "Sure, I might be able to help, can we chat next week?" If it's urgent for *you* to help but not urgent for them to keep in touch, you've got your answer.
- **Watch the Ratio** — Count how often they contact you without needing something. If the number is close to zero, so should your availability be.

How to Stop Being the Go-To Giver

1. **Say No Without a Ted Talk**

   You don't owe them an essay explaining why you can't help. "Sorry, I can't" is a complete sentence.

2. **Redirect to Neutral Ground**

Suggest a coffee catch-up that's purely social, no favours allowed. See if they still want to meet.

3. **Remove Yourself from the Rescue List**

    You're not an on-call lifeline for people who can't even remember your birthday.

Surviving Without Losing Your Sparkle

Not every favour is bad, and not every friend who needs help is using you. But when "Let's catch up" always translates to "I need you for something," you're not in a friendship, you're in a one-sided service arrangement.

And darling, you're not customer service.

You're the VIP guest list. Start acting like it.

Chapter 3:
The Selfie Friend
Who Only Calls in Good Lighting

(You're not a prop, darling, you're the whole show.)

You know the type. The "friend" who only pops up when there's a camera around, preferably at golden hour, in front of a latte art masterpiece, or while they're wearing a hat so wide it could pick up satellite channels.

They're not here for your soul, your stories, or your struggles.

They're here for the *aesthetic*.

And lucky you, you match their Instagram theme.

What Makes a Selfie Friend

Selfie friends treat life like a curated feed. If it's not photogenic, it's not happening. You're invited when you enhance the vibe, and mysteriously "forgotten" when you don't fit the mood board.

They'll drag you to rooftop bars, flower walls, and pop-up doughnut shops… but somehow can't return a text when you're home in sweatpants, dealing with a breakup.

Signs You're Just Their Human Filter

1. **The Friendship Is Geotagged**

    If all your memories together can be found under hashtags like #brunchgoals, but there's no trace of you during their bad days, you're a backdrop, not a bestie.

2. **The Posed Candids**

They'll insist "It's just a quick pic!" but somehow there's a tripod, a ring light, and five outfit changes in the car.

3. **The Disappearing Act Post-Photo**

   Once the content is captured, their enthusiasm deflates faster than a helium balloon on day two.

4. **You're Cropped When They Don't Look Good**

   In their world, your face is expendable, their angles are sacred.

Why They Do It

Selfie friends are often chasing validation, brand partnerships, or just the dopamine rush of likes. To them, people are part of the "content plan." The connection is secondary to the aesthetics.

How to Handle the Content Queen

1. **Ask for Real-Life Time**

    Suggest something that's not Insta-friendly — movie night, messy cooking session, rainy walk. If they're allergic to it, you have your answer.

2. **Stop Being Photo-Available on Demand**

    You're allowed to say no to being their unpaid photographer or co-star.

3. **See If They Check In Off-Camera**

    Do they message you when there's no event, no view, and no lighting? That's the friendship litmus test.

Surviving Without Losing Your Sparkle

Your worth isn't measured in how well you match someone's grid. Real friends want your presence, not your pixels.

The best moments in life aren't staged, they're messy, unfiltered, and usually involve laughter so ugly it can't be posted.

So next time the Selfie Friend calls, ask yourself:

Do they want *me*, or do they want *content*?

Because you're more than a caption, and your value doesn't need a filter.

Chapter 4:
How to Spot a Compliment Wrapped in a Jab

(Because sometimes "You look great" is actually "You looked terrible before.")

Fake friends love a good *complisult*.

It's the sneakiest way to cut you down while pretending to build you up. They'll smile sweetly, tilt their head, and drop a line that sounds kind… until it marinates in your brain for five minutes and you realise, they just called you ugly, lazy, or incompetent.

The Anatomy of a Complisult

1. **The Set-Up:** They start with sugar — something flattering, attention-grabbing, and disarming.
2. **The Hook:** They attach a sly qualifier, an unnecessary comparison, or a subtle dig.

3. **The Exit:** They leave you unsure whether to say "thanks" or challenge them, which means they win.

Example:

"Oh wow, you actually look really nice today!"

Translation: *You normally look like you wrestled a bin bag.*

Common Complisult Formats

- **The Backhanded Beauty Award:**

    "You look so pretty when you actually put in effort!"

    (Implying you're a swamp creature 80% of the time.)

- **The Disguised Critique:**

    "I wish I had your confidence to wear something like that."

    (Implying the outfit is a crime scene, but good for you for not caring.)

- **The Achievement Downplay:**

    "Congrats on your promotion! I didn't think they'd pick someone like you."

    (Ah, yes, the supportive shock of disbelief.)

- **The "You've Changed" Observation:**

    "You're so different now… in a good way!"

    (Implying you used to be terrible, and they're surprised you've evolved.)

Why They Do It

Complisults are often about control. It's a way for someone to plant a seed of doubt without looking like the villain. By couching criticism in sweetness, they keep their hands clean while still chipping away at your confidence.

Some do it to mask jealousy. Others do it because low-key undermining is their favourite sport. Either way, their goal is the same: to keep you in a position where you question yourself.

How to Spot the Hidden Jab

1. **Listen for Qualifiers** — "for once," "for you," "actually," "finally." These are red flag words in a compliment.
2. **Note Their Tone and Timing** — Do these comments come when you've achieved something, changed something, or just seem happy?
3. **Ask Yourself Who Benefits** — Does this "compliment" lift you up, or does it subtly put you back in your place?

How to Respond Without Losing Your Sparkle

- **The Graceful Deflect:**

    Smile and say "Thanks" without addressing the dig. (They hate not getting a reaction.)

- **The Playful Mirror:**

"Oh, I could say the same about you!" — said with just enough sweetness to make them wonder if you're joking.

- **The Direct Call-Out:**

    "That sounded like there was a dig in there — was that your intention?"

    (It's amazing how quickly people backtrack when caught.)

Surviving the Complisult Game

You can't stop people from serving you backhanded remarks, but you can stop letting them stick. Think of it like a badly wrapped gift; if it's ugly on the inside, you don't keep it just because the bow is pretty.

Real friends don't compliment you to knock you down.

They lift you without the fine print.

Chapter 5:
The Borrower
Who Forgets What They Borrowed

(Because your stuff isn't a community lending library.)

Some friends borrow sugar. Others borrow your hoodie, your charger, your car, your sanity... and somehow never return any of it.

You start out generous. It's "just for the weekend." Or "until payday." Or "until I find mine." Then weeks pass, months pass, and suddenly your favourite sweater has been spotted living its best life in their Instagram stories, on *them*.

The Borrower's Greatest Hits

1. **The "Oh, I Thought That Was Yours?" Amnesia**

They'll act genuinely confused, as if your property simply *migrated* into their home on its own.

2. **The Emotional Guilt Trip**

   "I would totally give it back, but my sister loves it and she's going through a hard time…"

   Translation: *We've adopted it now. Sorry about your loss.*

3. **The Constant 'I'll Bring It Next Time' Lie**

   "Next time" is the borrower's version of "the cheque is in the mail."

4. **The Upgrade Swap**

   They return your item… only after they've worn it out, broken it, or replaced it with something cheaper.

Why They Do It

Borrowers who never return things often live by the *Finders Keepers, Friendship Edition* rule. Sometimes it's entitlement ("We're friends, so what's yours is mine"). Sometimes it's poor boundaries. And sometimes, it's pure opportunism — they know you're too polite to chase them down.

How to Spot a Chronic Borrower

- **Their House Has a Suspicious Amount of Your Stuff**

    If you could furnish a small Airbnb with the items, they've "temporarily" borrowed, you have a problem.

- **They Always Ask for Things You Love**

    They don't want the backup bag; they want *the* bag.

- **Their Excuses Have a Netflix Original Plotline**

"Oh, your drill? It's in my cousin's shed… but the shed's in another town… and the key is at my ex's…"

How to Stop the Lending Loop

1. **Start with a Borrowing Ban**

    You're not being mean; you're protecting your peace (and your property).

2. **Label and Document**

    If you do lend something, take a photo of them holding it. Not for legal evidence, just so they know you're keeping tabs.

3. **Switch to "Use It Here" Rules**

    "You can absolutely borrow my blender… while you're in my kitchen."

4. **Ask Directly for Returns**

Don't soften it with "whenever you can." Try: "Hey, I need that back tomorrow."

Surviving Without Losing Your Sparkle

Your belongings are part of your life, your hard work, and your comfort, not a free-for-all for friends with sticky fingers and short memories.

Generosity is beautiful. Being taken for granted isn't.

And if they really value the friendship, they'll value your boundaries… and your blender.

The passive-aggressive chaos of digital friendships.

Chapter 6:
Group Chats
That Feel Like Hunger Games

(May the odds be ever in your favour… and may your notifications survive.)

Ah, the group chat, modern friendship's gladiator arena.

It starts as a wholesome way to "stay connected" and ends with unread message counts that rival your tax return anxiety.

Group chats can be a lifeline, a laugh factory, or a battlefield where sarcasm, passive-aggression, and GIF wars are the weapons of choice. One wrong emoji and suddenly you've triggered a three-day cold war.

The Cast of Characters in Every Hunger Games Chat

1. **The Ghost**

    Always "seen" but never speaks. Could be dead for all you know.

2. **The Over-Sharer**

    Sends 37 photos of their breakfast, their cat, and their bathroom renovation — before 9 a.m.

3. **The Drama Distributor**

    Drops explosive news and then goes offline like it's witness protection.

4. **The Event Pusher**

    Organises constant meetups but ghosts the chat when it's time to confirm attendance.

5. **The Sub-Tweeter in Text Form**

Posts vague quotes clearly aimed at one person in the group… but pretends it's "just something I saw on Pinterest."

Why Group Chats Go Toxic

When too many personalities collide in one thread, the group chat can morph from "fun updates" into a social survival challenge. Subtle alliances form, passive-aggressive tones emerge, and suddenly you're questioning if this is friendship or psychological warfare.

Signs You're in the Hunger Games Chat

- You dread opening it but also fear missing something important.
- "Hey guys" from certain people gives you fight-or-flight.
- You can feel the tension in the punctuation. ("Sure." vs "Sure!")
- Side chats have formed… about the main chat.

How to Survive Without Losing Limbs (or Friends)

1. **Mute Strategically**

   Notifications off. Sanity on. You're allowed to peek in on *your* schedule.

2. **Don't Take the Bait**

   If someone's fishing for a fight in a group chat, let them starve.

3. **Switch to One-on-One**

   If a message feels personal, address it privately; don't let the group become a gladiator pit.

4. **Exit Gracefully**

   "Hey guys, I'm trying to cut down on screen time, message me directly if you need me." Translation: *I'm leaving before this becomes the Roman Colosseum.*

Surviving Without Losing Your Sparkle

Group chats can be fun, but they can also be emotional minefields.

If it starts feeling less like friendship and more like alliance-building on reality TV, it's okay to log out.

Because in the group chat Hunger Games, the real victory is keeping your peace intact.

Chapter 7:
The Friend Who Loves You, Until You're Doing Better Than Them

(Because some people only clap for you when you're losing.)

At first, they're your ride-or-die. Your hype squad. Your number one cheerleader. They're the first to celebrate your small wins, the loudest voice in your corner… until you cross an invisible line, the one where your life starts to look a little shinier than theirs.

Suddenly, your achievements feel like crimes, your happiness feels like betrayal, and you can't quite pinpoint when the switch flipped.

The Jealousy Switch

This type of friend thrives when you're struggling, because it makes them feel needed, superior, or secure in their role. But once you're thriving, they start seeing you less as a friend and more as competition.

How It Shows Up

1. **The Disappearing Act**

    When you succeed, they "get busy" and can't be around to celebrate.

2. **The Downplay**

    "That's great for you, but anyone could have done it."

3. **The Comparison Game**

    They start one-upping your wins or finding ways to make your good news about them.

4. **The Sabotage Smile**

"I'm so happy for you!", followed by a passive dig or a story about why it won't last.

Why They Do It

Jealousy in friendship isn't always malicious. Sometimes it's insecurity — your success reminds them of what they haven't achieved yet. Other times, it's about control; if you're doing better, they fear losing relevance in your life.

But here's the truth: real friends don't need you to shrink for them to shine.

How to Protect Yourself

1. **Limit the Play-by-Play**

    You don't need to share every success with someone who can't celebrate without bitterness.

2. **Watch the Energy Exchange**

   Do they cheer you on when you're struggling but disappear when you're winning?

3. **Don't Shrink to Fit Their Comfort Zone**

   You've worked for your wins you're allowed to enjoy them without apologising.

4. **Upgrade Your Circle**

   Find people who see your success as proof that good things are possible for *everyone*.

Surviving Without Losing Your Sparkle

It's natural to want your friends to grow with you, but not everyone is capable of clapping when you're in the spotlight.

So, here's the rule:

If they only love you when you're losing, they don't deserve a seat at your victory table.

Chapter 8: When Every Story You Tell Becomes About Them

(You: "This is my moment." Them: "So anyway, here's my trauma.")

You start telling a story. It's *your* story.

Maybe you finally stood up to your boss, had an amazing date, or discovered you can make a pavlova without burning down the kitchen.

You get two sentences in…

And then, swoop! they hijack it like a conversational pirate.

Suddenly, you're the audience in a one-woman show you never bought tickets for.

The Story Thief's Signature Moves

1. **The Competitive Relate-Back**

   You: "I ran my first 5K!"

   Them: "That's cute, I ran a half marathon in the rain with a sprained ankle."

2. **The Sympathy Stealer**

   You: "I've been so stressed with work."

   Them: "You think *you're* stressed? My entire department was swallowed by a sinkhole."

3. **The Spotlight Grab**

   No matter the subject, holidays, heartbreaks, hangnails, they will find a way to make themselves the main character.

4. **The Interrupt & Redirect**

   They don't even wait for you to finish your sentence before starting theirs.

Why They Do It

Some Story Thieves are insecure and feel the need to compete for attention. Others genuinely lack self-awareness — they think they're "relating" when they're really just stealing your moment.

And for some, it's a subtle power move: if they control the narrative, they control the emotional energy of the conversation.

How to Spot the Hijack Early

- **Their Eye Contact Changes** — You can see them mentally loading *their* story before you've finished yours.
- **They Never Ask Follow-Up Questions** — Your story ends as soon as their story begins.
- **They "Yes, but" You** - Agreeing, then topping it instantly.

How to Reclaim Your Moment

1. **Politely Hold the Floor**

    "Hang on, I haven't finished, I promise I'll let you jump in after."

2. **Reinforce the Context**

    "That's interesting! But back to what I was saying…"

3. **Use the Mutual Spotlight Rule**

    Share the stage, but only with those who also give it back.

Surviving Without Losing Your Sparkle

It's not selfish to want your stories heard. Friendship is a two-way street, not an endless monologue.

You deserve friends who clap when it's your turn, listen without waiting to talk, and celebrate without needing to compete.

If they can't do that, they're not your conversation partner, they're your uninvited open mic act.

Chapter 9:
The Flaky Friend Olympics: Gold Medal Ghosting

(Because some people's commitment is as stable as a Jenga tower in an earthquake.)

We've all got one.

The friend who makes *big plans*, brunch, beach trips, maybe even that weekend getaway you were stupid enough to book in advance, only for them to pull a Houdini at the last second.

And not just once. Oh no. This is their *sport*.

Their personal Olympics.

And honey, they're undefeated.

The Flake's Event Schedule

1. **The Early Exit** — Cancels hours before because "I'm just sooo tired."
2. **The Strategic Delay** — Pushes it to "next week" indefinitely, like it's a Netflix show that will never get renewed.
3. **The Ghost Vanish** — Just doesn't show up. Doesn't text. Doesn't even *pretend* to care.
4. **The Excuse Marathon** — Elaborate tales involving car trouble, surprise guests, mysterious illnesses… yet somehow, they're tagged at another event that same day.

Why They Do It

Flaky friends often overcommit to look good in the moment, but when the time comes, they choose whatever's easiest, most fun, or most beneficial to *them*. Some have genuine anxiety or poor time management. Others simply don't value your time as much as their own.

The Warning Signs

- **They're "so excited" when plans are weeks away, but vague when the date gets close.**
- **They've never once initiated a plan you actually followed through on.**
- **Your calendar has more crossed-out events than completed ones because of them.**

How to Flake-Proof Your Life

1. **Go Low-Effort**

    Only plan things that won't ruin your day if they bail. Think coffee instead of concert tickets.

2. **Set the RSVP Trap**

    Confirm the day before and watch for the early signs of backpedalling.

3. **Stop Chasing**

    If they want to see you, they'll make it happen. If not, you've freed up your energy for people who will.

4. **Replace Them with Reliability**

   Your time is valuable. Spend it on friends who actually show up, physically *and* emotionally.

Surviving Without Losing Your Sparkle

The occasional cancellation is human. Chronic flaking is disrespect.

You don't need to compete for the attention of someone who treats plans like a suggestion. Let them win their invisible gold medal… and then let them do it without you.

Chapter 10: How to Avoid Becoming the Free Therapist

(Because your friendship isn't a 24/7 crisis hotline.)

Some friends don't just lean on you; they *move in* emotionally.

They texted at 2 a.m. about their ex.

They call on their lunch break to "vent" about their co-worker's breath.

They send voice notes longer than most podcasts.

At first, you're flattered. They trust you. They value your opinion. They think you're wise. But slowly, your life becomes a revolving door of other people's drama, and your own emotional tank hits empty.

The Emotional Dump Dynamic

- **They Offload, You Absorb** — Every problem they have becomes yours to fix (or at least, yours to carry).
- **They Rarely Ask About You** — If they do, it's a segue back to their own issues.
- **You Start Dreading Their Name on Your Screen** — Not because you don't care, but because you know it means work, not friendship.

Why It Happens

Some people don't know the difference between *sharing* and *dumping*. Others are addicted to validation and reassurance, and you've become their go-to source. And sometimes, you've trained them by always being available; you've shown them you're a free emotional buffet.

Signs You're the Friendship Therapist

1. **Your conversations are 90% about them.**
2. **They disappear when you need support.**
3. **You feel drained, not uplifted, after talking to them.**
4. **You've started Googling "how to fake your own death to avoid phone calls."**

How to Retire from the Role

1. **Set Time Boundaries**

    "I can chat for ten minutes, then I have to go." Keep it short and guilt-free.

2. **Redirect the Conversation**

    "That's a big one, maybe a counsellor could help you unpack that more deeply."

3. **Stop Playing Rescuer**

Offer empathy, not solutions. Let them do the emotional labour of solving their own problems.

4. **Space Out Responses**

   You don't have to reply immediately. Break the pattern of instant availability.

The Therapist Detox

If you've been the free therapist for years, expect resistance when you stop. They might accuse you of "changing" or "not caring." But remember: a real friend respects your limits.

You're allowed to care without carrying.

You're allowed to listen without absorbing.

And you're allowed to hang up.

Chapter 11: Your Secrets Are Not Group Currency

(If you wanted everyone to know, you'd have made a PowerPoint.)

Some friends can't hold water.

You tell them something in confidence a crush, a job offers, a medical diagnosis, and within 48 hours, it's been passed around like a bowl of chips at a party.

Suddenly, people you barely know are offering sympathy, advice, or *opinions you didn't ask for*. And you realise your friend didn't "accidentally" slip up... they traded your trust for attention, gossip, or the thrill of being the first to "know."

The Gossip Economy

In the wrong hands, secrets become currency.

Some people use them to buy closeness ("I'll tell you something if you tell me something"). Others use them for status ("I'm so in the loop"). And the worst kind? They use your secrets to make themselves look better, or make *you* look worse.

The Tell-Tale Signs

1. **The "Don't Tell Anyone, But…" Addict**

    Spoiler: if they say this to you, they're saying it to everyone else.

2. **The Fast Leak**

    You tell them something, and within hours, it's mysteriously "common knowledge."

3. **The Casual Slip**

"Oh, I didn't think it was a big deal to share!" Translation: *I knew exactly what I was doing.*

4. **The Competitive Confidante**

    They collect secrets from multiple people, then use them to pit friends against each other.

Why They Do It

Some do it for validation, being "in the know" makes them feel powerful. Others crave chaos and drama. And some are just careless, seeing your life as entertainment instead of something sacred.

How to Protect Your Secrets

1. **Test with Small Information**

Share something minor. If it comes back to you from another source, you know your answer.

2. **Go Need-to-Know**

   Not everyone needs access to every chapter of your life.

3. **Address the Leak Directly**

   "I heard you mentioned X to someone. That wasn't for sharing." No apologies, no softening.

4. **Revoke Access**

   Once someone shows you, they can't be trusted, stop giving them ammunition.

Surviving Without Losing Your Sparkle

Your private life is not community property.

A real friend knows that when you hand them a secret, you're handing them trust, and that's priceless.

So, keep your inner circle small, your boundaries strong, and your best stories for the people who treat them like treasures, not trading cards.

Chapter 12:
How to Survive Friends Who "Forget" to Invite You

(Spoiler: they didn't forget.)

There's a special sting in seeing your friends having a blast somewhere you weren't invited.

The group selfie on Instagram. The tagged location. The captions full of inside jokes you don't get because, surprise! you weren't there.

And when you ask, they hit you with the classic:

"Oh! We meant to invite you… we just forgot."

Darling, no. People don't forget to invite the people they *really* want there.

The Two Types of Uninviters

1. **The Accidental-But-Not-Really Forgetter**

   Claims it was an oversight, but somehow, you're left out more than you're included.

2. **The Strategic Social Curator**

   Chooses their guest list carefully for image, convenience, or control, and you didn't make the cut.

Why They Do It

Sometimes it's about group dynamics (they think you won't "fit" with the others). Sometimes it's selfish — they want a smaller group or a certain vibe. And sometimes, it's straight-up exclusion to remind you of your place in their social hierarchy.

The Telltale Signs It's Intentional

- **They Swear It Was Last-Minute**... but the event was clearly planned.
- **Other Mutual Friends Thought You'd Be There**... because you *should* have been.
- **It Happens Repeatedly** — one "forget" could be an accident. More than that is a pattern.

How to Handle It Without Begging for a Seat

1. **Stop Chasing Inclusion**

   If you have to fight for a spot, it's not worth being there.

2. **Make Your Own Plans**

   Build your own circle instead of trying to squeeze into theirs.

3. **Call Out Patterns, Not Incidents**

   "I've noticed I'm not included in a lot of things lately — is that intentional?" Watch them squirm.

4. **Reframe the Gift of Exclusion**

   Being left out means more time for people who *do* want you around.

Surviving Without Losing Your Sparkle

Not every door that closes is a loss — some are locked for a reason.

Real friends don't "forget" you. They think of you, they make space for you, and they want you there.

So, the next time someone "forgets" to invite you, don't wait at the door. Walk past it — and straight into a room where you're celebrated, not tolerated.

Chapter 13: Frenemies and Their Slow Drip Sabotage

(They're not stabbing you in the back… they're wearing you down drop by drop.)

Frenemies aren't the loud villains of your story — they're the quiet, smiling assassins. They know how to play the long game, eroding your confidence and credibility one tiny "innocent" move at a time.

They'll never do anything so obviously cruel that you can call them out without sounding paranoid. Instead, they use a tactic I call *slow drip sabotage*, tiny, repeated actions that weaken you until you start doubting yourself.

The Slow Drip Playbook

1. **The Micro-Dig**

"Oh, that's so *brave* of you to try that hairstyle."

2. **The Disappearing Credit**

    You come up with the idea, they present it as their own — and somehow people remember it as theirs.

3. **The Delayed Support**

    They "forget" to like, comment, or show up until it's too late for it to matter.

4. **The Subtle Sabotage in Front of Others**

    They share your embarrassing story "as a joke," or conveniently "misremember" details in a way that makes you look bad.

5. **The Controlled Access**

    They withhold important info, resources, or introductions, then act shocked when you miss out.

Why They Do It

Frenemies want to stay close enough to monitor your progress, but not so close that you surpass them. Keeping you a little insecure, a little off-balance, ensures you'll never feel fully solid in yourself — which is exactly where they want you.

How to Spot the Pattern

- You leave interactions with them feeling smaller, not bigger.
- They're warm one-on-one but undermine you in group settings.
- Their "advice" always seems to steer you away from your best interests.
- Good news seems to make them uncomfortable, even if they fake a smile.

How to Neutralise the Frenemy

1. **Stop Giving Them Ammo**

Keep personal wins, struggles, and plans to yourself.

2. **Go Public with Your Wins**

   Post your achievements so the credit is clear and can't be rewritten.

3. **Test Their Loyalty**

   Give them low-stakes opportunities to show up for you. If they fail, adjust your expectations permanently.

4. **Choose Your Distance**

   You don't have to cut them off completely, but they don't get VIP access to your life anymore.

Surviving Without Losing Your Sparkle

The beauty of slow drip sabotage is that it's quiet.

The power of catching it is that *you* can be even quieter while you shut off the tap.

Frenemies thrive in the shadows. Shine a light on their patterns, even if it's just in your own awareness, and you take away their favourite weapon: secrecy.

Chapter 14:
Social Media Stalkers
Disguised as Friends

(They don't call, they don't text, but they've seen every single one of your stories.)

They never comment. They never like. They never reach out to see how you're doing.

But post a story about your brunch? They're the first viewer.

Upload a photo with someone new? They've seen it within 14 seconds.

They are the *ghost lurkers* of your social media world, friends in title only, but silent watchers in practice.

The Stalker Friend Behaviour Guide

1. **The Early Bird**

Always first on your viewer list, no matter the time of day.

2. **The Breadcrumb Reactor**

   They don't interact with *you*, but they'll interact with people in your comments.

3. **The Offline Gossiper**

   Doesn't like your posts but mysteriously knows *everything* you've posted — and brings it up in person like they were there.

4. **The Watcher with an Agenda**

   Tracks your posts to gather intel on your relationships, job, or personal life — and then uses it for gossip or comparison.

Why They Do It

Some social media stalker-friends are just nosy. Others are keeping tabs because they want to monitor your life without the emotional labour of actually *being* in it. And then there are the jealous ones, who watch not to support you, but to measure themselves against you.

How to Tell It's More Than Casual Scrolling

- They never directly engage with you online, but they reference your posts in conversation.
- They know things you didn't tell them, because they saw it on your feed.
- They watch everything but contribute *nothing*.

How to Handle the Silent Watchers

1. **Adjust Your Privacy Settings**

   Limit your stories and posts to people who actually interact with you.

2. **Post Less About Your Personal Life**

   If they're using your posts as intel, give them nothing to work with.

3. **Call It Out Casually**

   "Oh, I didn't realise you saw that —you don't usually like my posts!"

4. **Accept Their Role**

   Not every follower is a friend. Some are just audience members — and you get to decide if they deserve a ticket.

Surviving Without Losing Your Sparkle

A view is not the same as support.

A follower is not the same as a friend.

And someone watching your every move from the sidelines isn't *in* your life, they're just peeking through the window.

Chapter 15:
How to Exit a Friendship Without Setting Yourself on Fire

(Because you can leave without burning the whole city down, or yourself in the process.)

Leaving a fake or toxic friendship isn't like unfollowing someone on Instagram. It's personal. Emotional. Messy. And if you've been friends for years, it can feel almost like a breakup, minus the flowers and heartfelt closure (and yes, sometimes without the maturity).

The trick is to protect yourself while making the cleanest possible exit. No explosions. No unnecessary drama. No emotional self-immolation.

Step 1: Decide If It's Really Over

Before you start cutting cords, be sure. Ask yourself:

- Have I communicated my boundaries clearly before?
- Have I given them a chance to show change?
- Does this friendship add anything good to my life anymore?

If the answer to that last one is a resounding *no*, it's time.

Step 2: Choose Your Exit Style

1. **The Slow Fade**

    Reduce calls, texts, and plans. Stop feeding the connection and let it naturally wither.

    Best for: Casual friends or people who don't notice much.

2. **The Direct Cut**

   Honest but calm conversation: "This friendship doesn't feel healthy for me anymore, and I need to step back."

   Best for: Long-term friendships or situations where they'll notice your absence.

3. **The Ghost**

   Total cut-off with no explanation.

   Best for: Dangerous, manipulative, or abusive situations where contact isn't safe.

Step 3: Keep It Drama-Free

- Don't recruit mutual friends to "your side."
- Don't post cryptic quotes on social media.
- Don't justify every little detail — the more you explain, the more they'll try to argue.

Step 4: Fortify Your Boundaries

They may try to guilt-trip you, rewrite history, or pull you back in. Decide your boundaries in advance:

- Will you respond to texts?
- Will you attend mutual events?
- Will you block them on social media?

Step 5: Replace the Void With Better Energy

Friendship breakups can leave you lonely. Fill the space with self-care, hobbies, and people who *do* respect and support you.

Surviving Without Losing Your Sparkle

Ending a friendship isn't betrayal, it's self-preservation.

You can walk away without setting yourself on fire to keep someone else warm.

And trust me, the air is cleaner on the other side.

Chapter 16:
The Energy Vampire Detox Plan

(Because you can't glow if they're sucking you dry.)

Energy vampires aren't the fanged, cape-wearing kind, but they'll leave you just as pale.

They're the people who drain your mood, your time, and your will to live, all while making it look like "just talking."

You don't notice it at first. You think you're being a good friend, a good listener, a good person. But slowly, your emotional battery is running on 2%, and every interaction with them feels like wading through wet cement.

The Energy Vampire Starter Pack

1. **The Crisis Addict**

   Always in an emergency, always expecting you to drop everything.

2. **The Negativity Black Hole**

   They have a problem for every solution, and your pep talks die on impact.

3. **The Drama Feeder**

   They thrive on chaos, and they want you front-row at every performance.

4. **The Passive-Needs Aggressor**

   Never asks directly, but guilts you into giving your time and attention.

Why They Do It

Some are lonely and lack healthy coping skills. Others are so self-focused that they treat people as portable emotional chargers. The problem? They never plug *anything* back into you.

Step 1: Identify Your Energy Leaks

After spending time with someone, ask yourself:

- Do I feel lighter or heavier?
- Do I feel heard or used?
- Am I looking forward to seeing them again, or dreading it?

Step 2: Set Energy Boundaries

- **Time Limits:** "I can chat for 15 minutes before my next thing."
- **Topic Limits:** Change the subject when they spiral.
- **Access Limits:** They don't get instant replies anymore.

Step 3: Rebalance Your Energy

1. **Bookend Vampire Encounters**

   Do something uplifting before and after seeing them to protect your mood.

2. **Increase Your Recharge Activities**

   Quiet time, hobbies, movement, rest — whatever fills you up.

3. **Surround Yourself With Givers**

   Spend more time with people who fill your cup instead of sipping from it.

Step 4: Cut or Contain

If boundaries don't work, you have two options:

- **Cut:** End the connection entirely.
- **Contain:** Reduce contact to the bare minimum needed.

Surviving Without Losing Your Sparkle

You can't shine if you're running on empty.

Protecting your energy isn't selfish — it's essential.

The truth is, you can't stop energy vampires from existing... but you *can* stop inviting them in.

Chapter 17: Boundary Bootcamp for People Who Hate Confrontation

(Because protecting your peace shouldn't feel like picking a fight.)

If the thought of setting a boundary makes you want to fake a bad Wi-Fi connection, you're not alone. For a lot of people, saying "no" feels rude, scary, or like you're about to ruin the friendship.

But here's the truth: boundaries aren't walls to keep people out — they're guardrails to stop you from driving off the cliff. And if you've been dealing with fake friends, you need those guardrails now more than ever.

Why Boundaries Feel Hard

1. **Fear of Conflict** — You imagine the conversation will blow up into drama.
2. **Fear of Rejection** — You worry they'll leave if you say no.
3. **People-Pleasing Programming** — You were raised to put everyone else first.

The Boundary Mindset Shift

A boundary isn't punishment. It's information. It tells people what's okay with you and what's not — so they can choose how to act.

Good friends adjust. Fake friends get offended. Either way, you get clarity.

Boundary Scripts for the Confrontation-Averse

- **The Polite Decline:**

    "Thanks for thinking of me, but I can't."
    (No explanation needed — though your inner people-pleaser will scream.)

- **The Time Guard:**

  "I can talk for 15 minutes, then I've got to run."

- **The Emotional Filter:**

  "I'm not in the right headspace to take that on right now."

- **The Repeat Offender Reset:**

  "I've mentioned this before — this isn't something I'm okay with."

The Three Rules of Boundaries

1. **Keep It Short** — The more you explain, the more room they have to argue.
2. **Stay Calm** — You're not asking permission, you're stating a fact.
3. **Hold the Line** — A boundary you don't enforce is just a suggestion.

Practise on Low-Stakes Situations

Try boundaries with strangers or acquaintances first — declining a store membership card, saying no to extra work, or telling a barista your order's wrong. Build your muscle before you need it for the big stuff.

Surviving Without Losing Your Sparkle

If someone respects you, they'll respect your boundaries.

If they don't, you've just learned something important about where they stand.

And the best part? The more you set boundaries, the easier they get, until "no" rolls off your tongue like you were born to say it.

Bonus Chapter: The Misunderstood People Pleaser

(Because wanting everyone to be happy doesn't make you the villain.)

People think people pleasers are sweet, harmless, and easy to get along with, until they don't.

Some see them as manipulative ("They're just being nice to get something"), others think they're weak ("They can't stand up for themselves"), and a few will even take advantage, knowing a people pleaser will rarely say no.

And here's the kicker, sometimes, people pleasers *do* accidentally cross into toxic territory, not out of malice, but because their fear of conflict or rejection twists their behaviour.

Why People Pleasers Get a Bad Rap

1. **The Hidden Resentment**

    When you say yes all the time but secretly wish you'd said no, that unspoken resentment leaks out.

2. **The Inconsistency**

    You'll bend over backwards for people you like, but avoid those you don't, and the contrast can look fake.

3. **The Perception of Manipulation**

    Over-giving can look like you're trying to "buy" approval, even if your heart is pure.

The People Pleaser's Internal Struggle

- **Fear of Disappointing Others** — The idea of someone being upset with you feels unbearable.

- **Identity Tied to Being Liked** — If you're not "the nice one," who are you?
- **Conflict Avoidance at All Costs** — Even if it costs *you*.

How to Keep People-Pleasing From Turning Toxic

1. **Check Your Motives**

    Ask yourself: "Am I doing this because I *want* to, or because I'm scared not to?"

2. **Say Yes With Boundaries**

    If you agree to something, set clear limits on your time, energy, and resources.

3. **Be Honest When You Can't**

    "I'd love to help, but I'm at capacity right now." It's kind *and* truthful.

4. **Stop Over-Apologising**

    Being polite doesn't mean apologising for existing.

For the People Dealing With a People Pleaser

Not all kindness is fake. Some people really *are* wired to care and help.

But if you notice someone saying yes to things they clearly resent, encourage them to be honest instead of punishing them for speaking up.

Surviving Without Losing Your Sparkle

Being generous, supportive, and kind is not toxic.

It's when you sacrifice your own needs, misrepresent your capacity, or hide behind niceness to avoid honesty that it can *look* toxic to others.

You can still be the helper, the carer, the one who shows up, just make sure you're showing up for yourself, too.

Chapter 18:
When Your "Bestie"
Is the First to Doubt You

(Because your number-one cheerleader shouldn't be your number-one sceptic.)

You share your big news.

You finally landed the job. You're starting the business. You've met someone amazing. You're booking the trip you've dreamed of for years.

And instead of excitement, your "best friend" gives you... hesitation.

The raised eyebrow. The "Are you sure?" The "That sounds risky."

They'll phrase it like concern, but underneath, it feels like doubt — heavy, uninvited, and chilling.

The Doubter's Greatest Hits

1. **The Risk Reminder**

    "That's great, but what if it doesn't work out?"

2. **The Devil's Advocate**

    Plays "just asking questions", all designed to poke holes in your confidence.

3. **The Dream Deflater**

    "Wow, that's... ambitious." Translation: *You're probably going to fail.*

4. **The History Throwback**

    Brings up old failures to "keep you realistic."

Why They Do It

Sometimes it's jealousy, your success threatens their comfort zone.

Sometimes it's projection, they can't imagine *they* could do it, so they assume you can't either.

And sometimes, it's control, keeping you small means keeping you close.

How to Tell It's Doubt, Not Concern

- **Pattern Over Time:** They question *every* dream you share, not just the risky ones.
- **No Follow-Up Support:** They never offer actual help or encouragement after the doubt.
- **Tone Over Words:** Concern feels warm. Doubt feels cold.

How to Protect Your Spark

1. **Share Selectively**

   Not everyone deserves front-row seats to your goals.

2. **Call It Out Gently**

   "I know you might mean well, but that felt more discouraging than supportive."

3. **Collect Real Cheerleaders**

   Surround yourself with people who push you forward, not hold you back.

4. **Separate Your Worth From Their Words**

   Their disbelief isn't your truth, it's their limitation.

Surviving Without Losing Your Sparkle

A best friend should be a safety net, not a cage.

If they're the first to doubt you every time, stop giving them the first word — and definitely don't give them the last.

The people who believe in you will clap the loudest. The rest can watch from the cheap seats.

Chapter 19:
How to Recognise Love Bombing in Friendships

(Because sometimes "You're my favourite person ever!" isn't as sweet as it sounds.)

When we think of love bombing, we usually picture romantic relationships — roses, over-the-top compliments, whirlwind gestures.

But fake friends can do it too, and in some ways, it's even more disarming.

They'll smother you with attention, praise, and loyalty — at first. They'll "adopt" you like you've been best friends forever. They'll text every day, hype you up constantly, and insist you're "basically family."

And then... once you're hooked? The switch flips.

The Friendship Love Bombing Playbook

1. **The Instant BFF**

   You've barely met, but they're already calling you their soulmate and planning matching tattoos.

2. **The Over-Investor**

   Wants to be involved in every part of your life immediately — your work, your hobbies, even your family drama.

3. **The Grand Gifter**

   Lavishes you with gifts, favours, and "let me pay for this" moments early on.

4. **The Constant Communicator**

   Messages non-stop, making you feel special and chosen — until they vanish.

Why They Do It

Friendship love bombing is about securing loyalty quickly. It's a shortcut to intimacy, designed to get you to trust them and prioritise them without question. But often, it's not sustainable. Once they've "got" you, the intensity fades, and the real dynamic emerges (usually manipulative, needy, or competitive).

The Crash After the Bomb

- They become distant or inconsistent, leaving you wondering what you did wrong.
- They start expecting you to meet the same level of effort they initially gave, even though *they've* stopped.
- They use your early trust to push boundaries or make demands.

How to Spot It Early

1. **Speed Test** — Real friendships grow gradually. If it feels like they're skipping stages, slow down.

2. **Balance Check** — Are they interested in *you*, or in how quickly they can integrate into your life?
3. **Consistency Watch** — Does their affection fade as soon as you're "secure" in the friendship?

How to Protect Yourself

- **Match Pace, Not Pressure** — Let the friendship build naturally, even if they push for more.
- **Hold Your Boundaries Early** — If they react badly to you saying no, that's your sign.
- **Don't Confuse Intensity with Stability** — The strongest friendships are steady, not overwhelming.

Surviving Without Losing Your Sparkle

Love bombing can feel magical in the moment, who doesn't want to feel adored? But the real magic is in the friends who show up for you with steady, reliable care long after the glitter fades.

The quick burn is exciting, but the slow burn is what keeps you warm.

Chapter 20:
The "One-Up" Friend Who Always Has It Worse or Better

(Because somehow, your story is never enough on its own.)

You start telling them about your week.

"I had the worst headache yesterday…"

Before you can even finish, they're off: "Oh, that's nothing, I had a migraine so bad last year I almost went blind."

Or maybe it's the opposite. You share a win.

"I finally got a pay rise!"

They nod, then casually drop: "Oh yeah, I got one too, mine was triple that, but good for you."

This is the *One-Up Friend*, the human competition machine. Every conversation is a scoreboard, and they have to be winning.

Two Flavours of One-Up Friend

1. **The Tragedy Toppers**

   Whatever you've been through, they've been through worse, and they'll tell you in graphic detail.

2. **The Bragging Bandits**

   Whatever you've achieved, they've done bigger, better, faster, shinier.

Why They Do It

One-upping is often about insecurity. They feel the need to prove their value by outshining or out-suffering others. It can also be about control — dominating the conversation keeps them in the spotlight.

How It Feels

- Your experiences feel dismissed or minimised.
- You start sharing less because you know they'll turn it into a contest.
- You leave conversations feeling smaller, not seen.

How to Handle a One-Upper

1. **Don't Play the Game**

   Resist the urge to one-up them back — it just fuels the competition.

2. **Redirect the Conversation**

   "That sounds intense, but back to what I was saying…"

3. **Limit Personal Sharing**

   If they can't respond without competing, keep your updates vague.

4. **Call It Out Lightly**

   "Wow, you always have a bigger version of my story!" Sometimes humour makes the point without a fight.

Surviving Without Losing Your Sparkle

A friend who needs to win every conversation isn't listening, they're performing.

And you don't owe them a stage.

The best friendships aren't about who's better or worse. They're about being in the trenches *and* on the podium together. If they can't do both, maybe it's time to leave them playing their game... alone.

Chapter 21:
When They Copy Everything but Your Struggles

(They want your crown, not your storms.)

Imitation is supposed to be the sincerest form of flattery... until it starts feeling like identity theft.

This is the friend who copies your clothes, your haircut, your hobbies, even your slang. They'll pick up the same lipstick shade, join the same gym, post in the same "authentic" tone on social media.

But here's the kicker — they only want the *highlight reel*.

The struggles that come with those wins? The long nights, the failed attempts, the hard work? Nope. Those get skipped. They just want the parts that make you look good — without any of the grind that got you there.

The Copycat Playbook

1. **The Instant Twin**

    You post a new outfit, they're wearing it within a week.

2. **The Hobby Hijacker**

    You start pottery, suddenly they're "obsessed" with clay work too.

3. **The Lifestyle Leech**

    You shift to a plant-based diet, they're suddenly "always been into it" — complete with an Instagram story about their "journey."

4. **The Rewrite Historian**

They retell *your* milestones as if they had them first.

Why They Do It

Copycat friends often crave the image you project but don't want to earn it. Sometimes it's jealousy in disguise — they figure if they can become you, they can compete with you. Other times, it's insecurity — they see you as a blueprint for being liked or admired.

The Problem

- It erases your individuality.
- It can make your hard-earned wins feel cheapened.
- It creates an undercurrent of competition instead of connection.

How to Handle the Copycat

1. **Protect Your Process**

    Share less about your behind-the-scenes so they can't shortcut it.

2. **Change Faster Than They Can Keep Up**

    Keep evolving. If they're always two steps behind, they'll never truly catch up.

3. **Call It Out Lightly**

    "Wow, we're twinning *again* — should I start invoicing you as a stylist?"

4. **Reclaim Your Narrative**

    Keep telling your story — people will know who started it.

Surviving Without Losing Your Sparkle

It's tempting to feel flattered by a copycat — at first. But over time, it can feel like you're being drained of originality.

Here's the truth: they can copy your clothes, your hobbies, even your captions… but they can't copy *you*.

The real magic isn't in what you do, it's in how you do it. And that's something they'll never be able to steal.

Chapter 22: The Coward's Apology and Why It Doesn't Count

(Because "sorry you feel that way" isn't an apology — it's a dodge.)

A real apology is simple:

"I'm sorry. I did this. It was wrong. I'll do better."

But fake friends don't deal in real apologies. They deal in coward's apologies, the kind that sidestep accountability, rewrite history, and somehow leave *you* feeling guilty.

The Greatest Hits of the Coward's Apology

1. **The "Sorry You Feel That Way"**

Translation: *Your feelings are the problem, not my actions.*

2. **The "If" Apology**

   "I'm sorry if you were offended."
   Translation: *I doubt you actually were, but here's a breadcrumb to shut you up.*

3. **The "Both Sides" Apology**

   "We both made mistakes." Translation: *I'm not taking full responsibility, so I'm spreading the blame around.*

4. **The "Timing Excuse" Apology**

   "I was just having a bad day."
   Translation: *I can be awful if I'm in a mood — deal with it.*

5. **The "Public Relations" Apology**

   Overly sweet and performative when others are watching, but flat and dismissive in private.

Why They Do It

Coward's apologies are about self-protection, not reconciliation.

They want to look like the bigger person without doing the actual work of admitting fault or making changes.

How to Tell It's Fake

- The focus is on your reaction, not their behaviour.
- They bring up *your* flaws mid-apology.
- Their actions don't change after "making amends."
- You leave the conversation more frustrated than before.

How to Respond

1. **Ask for Clarity**

"Are you apologising for what you did, or for how I feel?"

2. **Hold the Standard**

   Don't accept vague or blame-shifting statements as a resolution.

3. **Watch the Follow-Through**

   A real apology is backed by different behaviour; without that, it's just noise.

4. **Walk if Necessary**

   If they can't own their mistakes, they can't grow, and neither can the friendship.

Surviving Without Losing Your Sparkle

You don't have to accept half-baked apologies to keep the peace.

You deserve friends who can own their actions without turning it into a PR stunt.

Because a true friend doesn't just say "sorry", they make sure you don't need it again.

Chapter 23:
How to Stop Being Everyone's Emotional Dump Bin

(Because you're a person, not a landfill for feelings.)

Some friends treat you like the neighbourhood skip bin, they back up their emotional truck, dump everything inside, and drive off feeling lighter… while you're left sorting through the mess.

At first, you think you're being a good friend. You listen. You empathise. You try to help. But over time, you notice something — the dumping is all one way. They're never around when *you* need to offload.

The Dump Bin Dynamic

- **They Vent, You Absorb** — Every conversation feels like a therapy session you didn't agree to host.
- **No Emotional Reciprocity** — The moment you try to share, they change the subject or make it about them.
- **You Feel Drained, Not Connected** — Their relief comes at the cost of your peace.

Why It Happens

Some people genuinely don't realise they're doing it — they've gotten used to you being the "safe space." Others know exactly what they're doing and just don't care, because in their mind, you're built for emotional heavy lifting.

How to Recognise It Early

- You get anxious when you see their name pop up.
- Conversations feel one-sided and heavy.
- They never check in without following it with "Anyway, here's my crisis…"

How to Stop the Dumping

1. **Set Time Limits**

    "I can chat for ten minutes, but then I have to get back to things."

2. **Redirect the Energy**

    "That sounds like something a counsellor could help with."

3. **Require Balance**

    "Okay, you've shared your thing — now it's my turn."

4. **Don't Always Pick Up**

You're not on-call. Let some calls or messages go unanswered until *you* have the energy.

The "Clean-Up" Rule

If you leave an interaction feeling worse than you started, it's a sign to limit access next time. Protect your mental space like you would your physical home; you wouldn't let someone dump rubbish in your lounge room, so why let them do it in your head?

Surviving Without Losing Your Sparkle

Listening is a kindness. Being used as a dumping ground is exploitation.

The right friends will share *and* care, vent *and* listen, take *and* give.

You're allowed to close the lid.

Chapter 24: The Friend Who Shows Up Only for the Fun Stuff

(Because real friendship isn't just champagne and selfies.)

They're the life of the party. The plus-one to every brunch, BBQ, and beach day. They RSVP "yes" to dinners, festivals, and holidays faster than you can send the group chat invite.

But when the fun stops? When you're sick, stressed, moving house, or dealing with a breakup?

Suddenly, they're "so busy" or completely MIA.

The Fun Friend Formula

1. **Guaranteed Appearance at Social Highlights**

   Birthday? They're there. Baby shower? They'll bring a gift.

   Hospital visit? Crickets.

2. **High Energy, Low Depth**

   They're all laughs and cocktails, but when you need real support, they disappear.

3. **Selective Engagement**

   They'll "accidentally" miss serious conversations but be the first to suggest a night out.

Why They Do It

For some, it's about avoiding discomfort; they don't know how to handle hard emotions, so they just… don't.

For others, it's about convenience; if there's nothing in it for them, they're not interested.

The Problem

Friendship isn't a highlight reel. If they're only around for the good times, they're not a real friend; they're a social accessory.

How to Handle the Fun-Only Friend

1. **Adjust Your Expectations**

    Stop expecting them to be there for the hard stuff; they've already shown you they won't be.

2. **Match Their Level**

    Keep them as a "fun friend" if you enjoy their company, but don't give them deeper access than they've earned.

3. **Diversify Your Circle**

    Make sure you have people who show up *and* stay when things get tough.

4. **Don't Beg for Balance**

    If you have to convince someone to be there for you in hard times, they're not worth the effort.

Surviving Without Losing Your Sparkle

There's nothing wrong with having friends who are just for fun, as long as you don't confuse them with your inner circle.

Real friends show up for the champagne *and* the clean-up. The laughter *and* the tears. The highs *and* the lows.

Anyone else is just a guest star in your highlight reel.

Chapter 25: Why "No" Is the New Self-Care

(Because "yes" to them is often "no" to yourself.)

We're taught from childhood that "no" is rude, selfish, or mean.

Say "no" to a playdate, you're labelled unfriendly. Say "no" to helping, you're unkind. Say "no" to social plans, you're "anti-social."

But here's the truth: every time you say yes when you really want to say no, you're borrowing energy from your future self. And she's getting tired of the overdraft.

The Cost of Over-Yes-ing

- **Burnout** — Your schedule is full, but your soul is empty.
- **Resentment** — You start to dislike the people you keep helping, simply because you feel used.
- **Identity Loss** — You forget what *you* want because you're too busy keeping everyone else happy.

Why "No" Feels So Hard

1. **Fear of Disappointing People** — You want to be liked.
2. **Guilt Programming** — You were raised to think helping is your duty.
3. **Conflict Avoidance** — Saying yes feels easier in the moment.

The Self-Care Shift

"No" isn't rejection — it's redirection.

It's choosing to protect your energy, your time, and your mental health so you can actually show up fully when it *matters*.

How to Say "No" Without Apologising

- **Keep It Short:** "I can't." No justifying, no softening.
- **Offer an Alternative (If You Want):** "I can't tonight, but I'm free next week."
- **Use the Broken Record Method:** Repeat your no without adding new details for them to argue with.

The Magic of Selective Yes

When you save your yes for the things and people that truly matter, it becomes more valuable, and so do you.

Surviving Without Losing Your Sparkle

"No" is the ultimate self-care tool.

It's not a wall, it's a filter.

It keeps out the things that drain you, so you have space for the things that light you up.

And here's the best part: the people who respect you will respect your no. The ones who don't? That's your sign to say it again. Louder.

Chapter 26:
The Secret Test of True Friendship

(Because actions speak louder than "You know I'm always here for you.")

You don't need a staged betrayal scene to find out who's truly in your corner.

Sometimes, all it takes is a small, quiet test, nothing manipulative or mean, just a moment that lets people show you where they really stand.

True friends don't just say they've got your back, they *prove* it in the little ways, long before life throws you the big ones.

The Subtle Friendship Tests

1. **The Ask-and-Watch**

Request something small, a lift, help with moving a box, a quick favour, and see how they respond. A true friend will try to help if they can, not avoid eye contact.

2. **The Good News Drop**

   Share an achievement and watch their reaction. Do they light up with you… or look like they've swallowed a lemon?

3. **The Bad News Drop**

   Tell them something tough. Do they listen and support, or change the subject?

4. **The No-Test**

   Tell them no. Do they respect your boundary or guilt you into changing your answer?

5. **The Disappearing Act**

   Stop initiating for a while. See if they notice and reach out, or if the friendship dies on the vine.

Why This Works

Fake friends can fake big gestures when the audience is watching.

But consistency in the *small* things is harder to perform. These micro-moments expose whether the friendship is balanced, one-sided, or transactional.

How to Read the Results

- **They Pass:** You feel supported, seen, and valued without having to beg for it.
- **They Fail:** You feel drained, doubted, or like you're pulling all the weight.

And remember, if they fail one test, it's not instant exile. But if they fail most of them? That's your sign.

Surviving Without Losing Your Sparkle

The best part about the secret test is that it's quiet. No fights. No confrontations. Just you, collecting the data you need to decide who gets a front-row seat in your life.

Because friendship should be a safe space, not a guessing game.

Chapter 27:
How to Spot Jealousy in a Smile

(Because some "I'm so happy for you!" grins are really just gritted teeth.)

Not all smiles are created equal.

Some are warm and genuine, the kind that light up someone's whole face. Others? They're stretched too tight, held too long, or vanish the second you look away.

A fake friend will smile when you share your good news, but if jealousy's in the mix, their body will tell on them before their mouth does.

The Jealous Smile Checklist

1. **The Freeze Frame**

Their smile is delayed, like they had to process your news before forcing one out.

2. **The Tight-Lip Special**

   Lips pressed together, no teeth, it's the smile equivalent of a slow clap.

3. **The Smile-and-Switch**

   They smile for a split second before changing the subject away from your win.

4. **The Over compensator**

   They go *too* big with their grin, paired with a voice that's just a little too high-pitched. Overacting is a tell.

The Supporting Cast of Jealousy

The smile is just the headliner, watch for these other micro-reactions:

- **Eye Flick:** Their gaze shifts down or away mid-congratulations.
- **Tone Drop:** Their voice loses warmth by the end of the sentence.
- **Mini Sigh:** A barely-there exhale right after your news.

Why They Do It

Jealousy is natural — but in a healthy friendship, it's overshadowed by pride and support. In a fake friendship, jealousy wins. The smile is their attempt to hide it… but human body language is terrible at keeping secrets.

How to Respond Without Losing Your Sparkle

1. **Stay Confident**

    Don't shrink your win to make them comfortable.

2. **Change the Energy**

If you sense tension, steer the convo somewhere lighter; you're not there to coach them through their feelings.

3. **Take Mental Notes**

   If their smile never feels genuine, it's a pattern worth paying attention to.

Surviving Without Losing Your Sparkle

The way someone reacts to your success is one of the clearest indicators of their true feelings toward you.

If the smile is real, you'll feel it. If it's fake, you'll sense it — and now you know exactly what to look for.

Chapter 28: The Friend Who Turns Into a Stranger Overnight

(Because sometimes the scariest ghosting is from someone who's still alive and active on Instagram.)

One day you're swapping memes, sharing secrets, and making plans.

The next? Silence.

No fight, no fallout, no explanation, just a sudden, icy shift like they've erased you from their contacts… but kept you on their story viewer list.

It's confusing. It's painful. And it can feel worse than an actual breakup because you don't even know *why*.

The Overnight Stranger Pattern

1. **The Sudden Chill**

    Messages go from enthusiastic paragraphs to curt one-liners.

2. **The Plan Evaporation**

    They stop inviting you to things you used to do together.

3. **The Public Silence**

    They're active online, maybe even engaging with mutual friends, but you're invisible to them now.

4. **The Memory Wipe**

    They act like your shared history barely existed, no warmth, no nostalgia, just… distance.

Why It Happens

- **They've Replaced You** — A new friend group or relationship took priority.
- **They Can't Face a Conversation** — Confrontation makes them uncomfortable, so they just disappear.
- **They're Avoiding Accountability** — Maybe they hurt you or know they'd have to admit fault.
- **It's About Them, Not You** — Internal issues, mental health struggles, or burnout — but instead of saying that, they just vanish.

The Emotional Fallout

This kind of ghosting leaves you stuck in limbo, replaying every interaction, wondering what you did wrong. The truth? You may *never* get closure from them — so you have to give it to yourself.

How to Handle It

1. **Don't Chase**

   If someone wants to leave, let them. Clinging only prolongs the pain.

2. **Resist Self-Blame**

   Unless there was a specific, known conflict, their silence is about their own limits — not your worth.

3. **Fill the Gap With Supportive People**

   Replace the dead air with voices that value and uplift you.

4. **Decide If You'd Even Let Them Back In**

   If they returned tomorrow, would you trust them again? Answer honestly.

Surviving Without Losing Your Sparkle

Sometimes the hardest part of losing a friend isn't the loss itself — it's the *uncertainty*.

But here's the truth: real friends don't turn into strangers overnight.

If they can cut you off that easily, they were never as close as you thought. And if they can leave without a word, you can live without their noise.

Chapter 29: Emotional Hoarders: They Take, Never Give

(Because friendship is not a self-service buffet where you're the only dish.)

Some friends are like storage units for emotional support, they'll take *all* of yours, cram it into their lives, and never return any of it.

They're the first to call when they need a pep talk, validation, or someone to listen to their late-night rants… but when you need an ear, a favour, or even just a "how are you?", nothing.

It's not that they're bad at friendship. It's that they've redefined it in their head: you're their supplier, and they're the customer.

The Emotional Hoarder Checklist

1. **The Constant Collector**

   They gather sympathy, advice, and attention like it's going out of style.

2. **The Conversation Black Hole**

   Every chat gets sucked into their life, their problems, their stories — yours vanish.

3. **The Seasonal Friend**

   They pop up when they need something and vanish once they've got it.

4. **The Zero-Return Policy**

   No matter how much you've given, don't expect the favour back.

Why They Do It

Some emotional hoarders are self-centred by nature. Others have gotten used to being carried by people who don't push back. And some genuinely don't *see* the imbalance because they've never been told no.

The Problem

Over time, you become depleted. It's not just the imbalance — it's the message it sends: *your needs don't matter here.*

How to Handle an Emotional Hoarder

1. **Track the Balance**

    Notice how often they check in without an agenda. If the answer is "never," adjust accordingly.

2. **Limit Your Availability**

    Just because they call doesn't mean you have to answer.

3. **Ask for What You Need**

   "I've been supporting you a lot lately, can I get your thoughts on something going on for me?"

4. **Shift the Dynamic or Step Back**

   If they can't meet you halfway, it's time to spend your energy elsewhere.

Surviving Without Losing Your Sparkle

Friendship is supposed to be a give-and-take — not a take-and-take.

If you feel like an emotional landfill instead of a loved friend, it's not selfish to close the gates.

Because your energy is precious, and you deserve friends who know how to give it back.

Chapter 30:
What to Do When They Choose Sides Against You

(Because loyalty shouldn't be optional.)

Few things sting like a friend choosing someone else over you in a conflict, especially when they know the truth, know your heart, and know how much their choice will hurt.

Whether it's a petty argument, a major falling out, or straight-up lies being spread about you, the betrayal isn't just that they didn't defend you; it's that they *aligned* with someone who wouldn't hesitate to hurt you.

Why It Hurts So Much

- **It's Personal** — They didn't just pick a side; they picked *against* you.

- **It Questions Your History** — If they can drop you this easily, were they ever really on your team?
- **It Shatters Trust** — Even if they come back, you'll never look at them the same way.

The Side-Picker Playbook

1. **The "I Don't Want to Get Involved" Hypocrite**

    Says they're staying neutral but somehow ends up hanging out more with the other side.

2. **The Opportunist**

    Sides with whoever benefits them socially, financially, or emotionally in the moment.

3. **The Secret Gossip**

    Pretends to support you privately while feeding the other side information.

4. **The Public Defender — For Them**

Goes out of their way to defend the person who hurt you, while staying silent for you.

Why They Do It

Side-picking is often about self-preservation — they want to keep the peace for themselves, even if it means sacrificing you. Other times, it's about convenience, social positioning, or revealing that their loyalty was never that deep to begin with.

What to Do When It Happens

1. **Don't Beg for Loyalty**

   If someone has to be convinced to stand by you, they're not loyal.

2. **Take a Step Back**

   Distance yourself before the hurt turns into bitterness.

3. **Protect Your Story**

Stop sharing personal details they could twist or leak.

4. **Strengthen Your Circle**

   Invest in people who have *proven* they'll stand beside you, even when it's inconvenient.

The Closure Truth

You may never know exactly why they chose the other side, but you *do* know this:

Real friends don't just stand by you in the sunshine. They stand in the storm, even if it means getting wet.

Surviving Without Losing Your Sparkle

Loyalty isn't about always agreeing, it's about having each other's backs, even when things get messy.

If they can't do that, you're better off without them in your corner.

Because losing a fake friend is painful, but keeping them is worse.

Chapter 31: Friend Breakups Hurt Worse Than Boyfriend Breakups (and How to Heal)

(Because losing your person is a different kind of heartbreak.)

Romantic breakups get all the headlines the sad songs, the ice cream binges, the tearful phone calls to your bestie. But when the *bestie* is the one you lose? That heartbreak hits differently.

A friend breakup isn't just the end of a relationship, it's the end of the person you trusted with your secrets, your history, your unfiltered self. You don't just lose them... you lose the *home* you had in them.

Why It Hurts So Much

- **They Knew Everything** — Your fears, your wins, your flaws.
- **They Were in Every Corner of Your Life** — Work, family, holidays, random Tuesday memes.
- **There's No Rulebook** — With romantic breakups, there's an expected process. Friend breakups? You're left to figure it out alone.

The Emotional Stages of a Friend Breakup

1. **Shock** — How can they just… not be here anymore?
2. **Confusion** — Replaying every moment, searching for where it went wrong.
3. **Anger** — How dare they treat you like you were disposable?
4. **Grief** — Mourning the shared history and the person you thought they were.
5. **Acceptance** — Realising you can love the memories and still move forward without them.

How to Heal Without Losing Your Sparkle

1. **Allow the Grief**

    Don't minimise it, it *is* a loss, and it deserves to be grieved.

2. **Write the Goodbye Letter You'll Never Send**

    Get the words out so they stop swirling in your head.

3. **Detox Your Triggers**

    Mute or unfollow them on socials. Pack away photos until you're ready.

4. **Fill the Space with Joy**

    New hobbies, new people, solo adventures — remind yourself you're more than this friendship.

5. **Rebuild Trust Slowly**

    The end of one friendship doesn't mean every friendship will end the same way.

The Perspective Shift

Sometimes the end of a friendship isn't the end of your story; it's the clearing of space for better, more aligned people to come in.

People who will love you for who you are now, not just who you were when you met.

Surviving Without Losing Your Sparkle

A friend breakup may feel like the end of an era, but it's also the start of one where you know yourself better, protect your energy more fiercely, and only let in people who treat your heart with care.

Because love isn't just romantic. And losing it isn't just about relationships. Sometimes, the deepest love we lose is platonic, and the deepest healing is learning we can survive without it.

Chapter 32:
The Long Game of Letting Go

(Because some people take longer to leave your heart than they did to leave your life.)

Letting go sounds simple.

Delete the number. Unfollow the socials. Stop texting first.

But the truth? Letting go is rarely one clean cut — it's a slow, messy process that happens in layers.

You'll think you're over them, and then a song, a smell, or a photo will crack the door open in your mind again. And that's okay. Healing doesn't have to be instant to be real.

Why Letting Go Takes Time

- **Your Brain Misses the Familiar** — Even bad friendships can feel safe because you know their rhythms.
- **Memories Aren't Just Bad** — Mixed memories make it harder to detach, because you can't hate them completely.
- **You're Grieving the "What Could Have Been"** — The future you imagined with them still lingers in your mind.

The Layered Let-Go Method

1. **Physical Distance First**

   Reduce contact, unfollow, or mute, stop feeding the daily habit of them in your life.

2. **Emotional Detangling**

   Stop replaying the good moments without remembering why it ended. Balance the nostalgia with the reality.

3. **Reclaim the Spaces**

If you used to do certain things together, brunch spots, hobbies, routines, reclaim them solo or with new people.

4. **Release the Narrator Role**

   Stop telling the story of what happened over and over. Each retelling keeps them alive in your present.

5. **Fill the Gap With Growth**

   New friends, new projects, new adventures — don't just subtract, add.

The Patience Factor

You won't wake up one day completely over it. But you *will* wake up one day and realise you've gone a week without thinking about them... then a month... and eventually, they'll just be a chapter in your book, not the headline.

Surviving Without Losing Your Sparkle

Letting go isn't about hating them or wishing them harm. It's about reclaiming the space in your heart and mind that was crowded by their absence.

You don't have to rush it. You just have to keep walking forward, even if some days, it's only a step.

Chapter 33: Your Next Best Friend Might Be You

(Because the most loyal person you'll ever have in your corner is already in your mirror.)

We spend so much energy searching for that one friend who "gets" us, who will always be there, never judge, always listen, and cheer us on without competition.

But here's a wild truth: that friend can be *you*.

When you stop chasing the approval of people who can't (or won't) show up, you make space for the one person who's been quietly waiting for your attention all along, yourself.

Why Being Your Own Best Friend Matters

- **You Set the Standard** — When you treat yourself well, you stop tolerating less from others.
- **You're Always Available** — No time zone, mood swing, or flaky calendar can take you away from yourself.
- **You Build Emotional Safety** — You can trust you won't betray your own boundaries.

Ways to Be the Friend You Need

1. **Celebrate Your Wins**

   Don't wait for someone else to clap — be your own standing ovation.

2. **Keep Your Own Secrets**

   Protect your vulnerabilities like they're priceless (because they are).

3. **Show Up Consistently**

Commit to your own well-being the way you've committed to everyone else's.

4. **Talk to Yourself Like You Would a Loved One**

   No insults, no self-sabotage, just honesty and encouragement.

The Ripple Effect

When you build that strong, loving friendship with yourself, you naturally attract people who treat you the same way. You also become better at spotting those who don't — and walking away faster when they show you, they can't meet your standard.

Surviving Without Losing Your Sparkle

You are not half a person waiting to be completed by someone else's friendship. You are whole, valuable, and worthy all on your own.

So, if you've just walked away from fake friends, remember this: your next best friend might not be a stranger you haven't met yet... it might be the person who's been with you through *everything*.

You.

ACT 2 – The Family Circus

Being the black sheep without being trampled.

Chapter 34:
When Family Feels Like a Full-Time Job You Didn't Apply For

Some people get job offers with welcome packs, paid leave, and onboarding sessions. You? You got handed a birth certificate and a lifetime contract that doesn't even come with coffee breaks.

Being part of a family can feel like working in a chaotic start-up that never quite figures out its business plan. The roles aren't clearly defined, the rules keep changing, and your boss (who may or may not be your mother) thinks "boundaries" is a dirty word. You're expected to be the unpaid therapist, the emotional punching bag, the events coordinator, and occasionally the emergency loan provider, all while being told you should be grateful to be part of the team.

Here's the kicker: family *loves* to act like these are "just normal family responsibilities." Translation: they need you to do the work so they can keep doing what they've always done, with zero self-awareness and a touch of guilt-tripping flair.

So how do you survive the job you never applied for?

1. Start Tracking Your Overtime

You don't need a timesheet but notice how often you're on call. How many late-night phone calls do you take? How many emotional fires are you expected to put out? Awareness is your first step to change.

2. Write Your Own Job Description

You can't change the whole system, but you *can* define what you are (and aren't) willing to do. "I'm not the family's last-minute babysitter" is a perfectly valid position statement.

3. Stop Attending Every Meeting

You're not obligated to show up to every family gathering, especially if they leave you emotionally drained for days. Declining is not betrayal, it's self-preservation.

4. Introduce Boundaries Like Policies

Think of boundaries as company policies. Clear, firm, and non-negotiable. If they don't like the new rules? That's a *them* problem, not a *you* problem.

5. Remember: You Can Quit

You don't have to fully cut ties to take a step back. Scaling down your "hours" is not cruel, it's how you keep your sanity. If you were in an actual toxic workplace, you'd leave without question. Your peace is worth the same.

At the end of the day, family should be a source of love and support, not unpaid labour. And if yours feels more like a relentless grind, you have every right to put down the phone, lock the metaphorical office, and take a holiday, starting today.

Chapter 35:
The Difference Between Boundaries and Betrayal

Here's the problem: when you start setting boundaries with family, a certain breed of relative will look at you like you just stabbed Grandma's antique china collection.

They confuse *boundaries* with *betrayal*. In their mind, saying "no" is the same as saying, "I no longer love you and I wish you nothing but ruin." Which is ridiculous — you can love someone and still not want them bulldozing through your personal space like an emotional excavator.

Let's get one thing straight:

Boundaries are *not* about punishment. They're about protection, yours.

1. Boundaries Say: "I Care About My Mental Health"

Betrayal says: "I'm going to hurt you on purpose."

Big difference. Boundaries are an act of self-respect. They prevent burnout, resentment, and the quiet seething that eventually leads to you screaming in the bathroom at Christmas lunch.

2. The Pushback Is Proof They Worked

The louder they protest, the more necessary the boundary was. Think of it like baby-proofing your house — the baby will cry when you block off the staircase, but you're still not going to let them tumble down.

3. Boundaries Benefit Them, Too

They may never admit it, but when you set limits, you're teaching them how to treat people better. One day, they might even thank you. (Probably not. But maybe.)

4. Reframe the Narrative

Instead of thinking, *I'm letting them down*, try, *I'm teaching them how to treat me right*. You're not betraying the family — you're breaking a toxic cycle.

5. When All Else Fails, Repeat This Mantra

"A lack of boundaries invites a lack of respect."

If someone truly loves you, they'll learn to live within your limits. If they can't, then what they loved wasn't *you*, it was the version of you who overextended herself for their comfort.

Bottom line? You're not the villain in their soap opera. You're the scriptwriter, and you've just cut the scenes where they trample all over you. That's not betrayal, that's editing.

Chapter 36:
Why "That's Just How They Are" Is Gaslighting in Disguise

If you've ever tried to call out bad behaviour in a family setting, chances are you've been hit with the magic phrase:

"Oh, that's just how they are."

And just like that, you're expected to swallow your feelings, accept their treatment, and carry on as if Aunt Judy didn't just torch your self-esteem over potato salad.

Let's be clear: *that* phrase is not harmless. It's a velvet-covered hammer designed to shut you down. It reframes the problem as *your* inability to tolerate someone, instead of acknowledging that their behaviour is actually awful.

1. It's Permission Slipped in Disguise

When someone says, "that's just how they are," what they're really saying is: *We've decided they're allowed to be toxic because it's easier than asking them to change.* It's a family hall pass for bad behaviour.

2. It Puts the Responsibility on You

Rather than holding the person accountable, you're expected to "manage" them, which usually means walking on eggshells, over-explaining yourself, or pretending their barbs don't land.

3. It Normalises the Unacceptable

Over time, everyone just *accepts* the behaviour like it's part of the furniture. Uncle Dave's casual cruelty? "That's just Dave." The sibling who competes with you over everything? "That's just her way." No. That's just them refusing to grow up.

4. It Trains You to Shrink

When a family repeatedly excuses someone's behaviour, you learn to make yourself smaller to avoid conflict. This is survival mode, not healthy family dynamics.

5. The Reality Check

Here's the truth bomb:

"That's just how they are" is not a reason. It's an excuse.
And excuses are the enemy of change.

How to Flip the Script:

Next time someone tries that line, try responding with:

"And this is just how I am, I have boundaries."

They might choke on their tea, but you'll sleep better at night.

You are not obligated to accept bad behaviour just because it has a long history. If anything, long histories are *more* reason to stop the cycle. Otherwise, you're not keeping the peace, you're keeping the problem.

Chapter 37: The Family Member Who Always Keeps Score

You know that one relative who remembers *exactly* how many times they've done something for you, and exactly how many times you haven't returned the favour?

They don't give gifts, they make investments. And those "investments" come with an interest rate so high, you'd be better off taking a loan from the mob.

1. Nothing Is Ever Free

When they help you, it's not kindness. It's a transaction. And they'll keep the receipt forever. That Christmas, they "lent" you their spare room for a week? They'll bring it up every Easter until the end of time.

2. Your Wins Are Their Losses

The scorekeeper isn't happy when you're happy. They're busy recalculating the balance sheet in their head. If you succeed, they mentally add up all the ways they think you "owe" them credit.

3. They Weaponise the Ledger

These relatives have a magical ability to recall events from 15 years ago in crystal-clear detail, but only if it benefits them. Your side of the story? Mysteriously missing from their mental archive.

4. Why They Do It

Keeping score is about control. If they can keep you in their emotional debt, they can make you feel guilty enough to keep doing what they want. It's manipulation dressed up as "memory."

5. How to Win the Game (By Not Playing)

The only way to beat a scorekeeper is to step off the playing field entirely. That means:

- Stop accepting favours you don't actually want.
- Give freely without expecting anything in return, but don't give to them if it always comes back with strings attached.
- When they bring up the past, refuse to engage in the "you owe me" conversation.

Boundary Script:

"I appreciate when you've helped me, but I'm not going to keep a running tally. If you're only doing things to keep score, I'd rather we skip it."

Yes, they'll be offended. No, you're not the bad guy. You're just declining to live under emotional accounting rules that benefit only them.

You don't need to win their game. You just need to quit playing. And spoiler alert: once you stop keeping score with them, you'll have a lot more emotional energy to spend on people who *actually* care about you.

Chapter 38:
How to Stop Explaining Yourself to People Who Don't Listen

If you've ever found yourself in a three-hour conversation explaining why you *don't* want to go to Aunt Linda's "mandatory" family BBQ, only for Aunt Linda to reply, "So, what time will you be there?", you already know the pain.

1. The Illusion of Logic

You think if you explain your reasoning clearly enough, they'll *get it*. But you're dealing with someone who's not missing the *information*; they're missing the *respect*.

2. Listening vs. Waiting to Talk

A true listener processes your words. A fake listener just sits there rehearsing their rebuttal in their head until you shut up so they can deliver it. They're not having a conversation; they're holding court.

3. Over-Explaining Is a Trap

Every extra detail you give becomes ammunition.

- "I can't come because I'm working." → "But it's just one day."
- "I'm exhausted." → "Well, you'll be sitting down most of the time."
- "I have plans." → "Bring your plans here."

4. The Truth They Don't Want to Hear

They're not confused. They're not misunderstanding you. They're ignoring you, because your boundaries inconvenience them.

5. Your New Rules

- **Say it once.** You're not Netflix, you don't do reruns.
- **Cut the "because."** You don't owe them a dissertation.
- **Let silence work.** When they push, resist the urge to fill the gap. Let them sit with your answer.

Boundary Script:

"I've already told you my decision. I'm not explaining it again."

You'll feel mean the first time you do it. Then you'll feel free.

Because here's the thing: every time you explain yourself to someone who's not listening, you're giving away power. And you can spend that power on building a life you love, or you can waste it trying to get someone to hear a message they've already decided to ignore.

Chapter 39: When Your Achievements Are Met with Silence

You worked for it. You sacrificed for it. You finally hit the goal, and your family reacts like you just told them you found a new brand of dish soap.

1. The Sound of Jealousy

Some people can't celebrate you because your win reminds them of their lack of effort. Your promotion, your new apartment, your degree, it's proof that the excuses they've been clinging to aren't unbreakable chains; they're just choices.

2. The Shapeshifting Response

When they do say something, it's never a straight-up "Congratulations."

- **The Downplay:** "Oh, anyone can do that if they try hard enough."
- **The One-Up:** "Well, when I was your age…"
- **The Deflect:** "Must be nice. Anyway, did you hear about"

3. Why Silence Hurts More Than Criticism

Criticism at least acknowledges that you *did* something. Silence tries to erase the fact it ever happened — because they can't handle the spotlight not being on them.

4. What You Do About It

- **Stop waiting for applause.** You're not a circus act.
- **Tell the right audience.** Some people are allergic to joy, find people who aren't.

- **Remember the scoreboard.** Their silence says nothing about your achievement, but everything about their character.

5. Power Move

Treat their silence like approval.

- "Thanks for noticing!" with a smile.
- Or better yet, keep living like you're the headline, because you are.

Chapter 40: The Relative Who Needs You but Can't Stand You

They talk about you behind your back. They roll their eyes at family dinners. But the second they need help moving a fridge, suddenly you're their favourite person.

1. The Hypocrisy Hall of Fame

These relatives operate on a cycle:

1. **Dislike you loudly.** (Gossip, criticism, subtle digs.)
2. **Need something from you.** (A favour, money, a "quick" lift that's somehow 90 minutes away.)
3. **Act like nothing ever happened.** (Because acknowledging it might mean apologising, and we all know that's not happening.)

2. Why They Do It

It's not that they *like* you when they need you — it's that they like what you can *do* for them. You're a convenience, not a connection.

3. How to Spot Them Early

- Their compliments come with a request attached.
- They "forget" past drama when they want something.
- They get mysteriously warm and friendly right before asking for a big favour.

4. How to Handle It Without Losing Your Mind

- **Stop rewarding bad behaviour.** Help only when *you* want to, not because you feel guilty.
- **Use the broken record method:** "Sorry, I can't help with that." (Repeat as necessary.)

- **Put your time where it's valued.** If they can't stand you, they can't borrow you either.

5. Power Move

If you *do* help, make it transactional. "Sure, I can do that, it's $50 for my time and petrol." Watch how quickly they find someone else.

Needing you and disliking you is their problem, not your personality flaw. You're not here to be their unpaid Uber with a side of emotional punching bag.

Chapter 41: Holidays Without the Drama (Yes, It's Possible)

Holidays are supposed to be about joy, gratitude, and stuffing yourself with enough food to question your life choices. But for some families, it's just a seasonal reminder that certain people should never be in the same room, especially with wine involved.

1. Know Your Triggers Before They Arrive

- *Uncle Bob and his "jokes"* → assign him to the kids' table far away from you.
- *Your mother's critique of your life choices* → prepare one neutral but final response.
- *The cousin who starts political debates* → "Oh look, the pavlova's ready!" and change the subject.

2. Control What You Can

- If you're hosting, **control the guest list**. Strategic invites are self-care.
- Set **start and end times** — because "lingering" is where the drama brews.
- Make a "Drama-Free Zone" rule; political rants, gossip, and "When are you having kids?" questions are banned.

3. If You're the Guest

- Arrive late, leave early.
- Bring your own escape plan (yes, "I have to feed my cat" works, even if you don't own a cat).
- Keep your drink in hand, both as a shield and an excuse to exit conversations.

4. Pre-Game Your Boundaries

Practice your polite shutdown lines:

- "Let's talk about something lighter."
- "I don't feel like discussing that right now."
- "I'm here to enjoy the holiday, not debate."

5. Create New Traditions

Sometimes the healthiest choice is skipping the traditional family gathering altogether and starting your own version with friends, your chosen family, or just Netflix and takeout. There's no rule that says you have to celebrate in a war zone.

Bottom Line

A drama-free holiday isn't about changing other people, it's about protecting your peace, even if that means skipping the table entirely. Remember: presence is a gift, but it's *your* gift to give

Chapter 42: The Gossip Mill That Runs on Your Business

Some families have a loving tradition of sharing recipes. Others? They share *your private life* like they're auditioning for a job at TMZ.

The family gossip mill is not just a casual chat — it's a **full-scale operation**. Information is gathered, exaggerated, and redistributed faster than you can say, "Please don't tell anyone."

1. Recognise the Types of Gossipers

- **The Town Crier** – Delivers your news *immediately* to the entire extended family, with a few dramatic flourishes.
- **The Whisperer** – Pretends to keep your secret but tells "just one person" (which is somehow everyone).

- **The Historian** – Brings up every mistake you've ever made in chronological order for added impact.

2. Stop Supplying the Headlines

If you don't want it shared, **don't say it**, even "in confidence." Some people think "confidential" means "start typing."

Practice the art of vague answers:

- "Things are fine."
- "I'm working on a few things."
- "Oh, you know… life."

3. Redirect the Story

If someone tries fishing for gossip, flip it:

- "That's boring, tell me what's going on with *you*."
- "I heard you've been busy lately, spill."

4. Use the "Misinformation Strategy" (Optional, but Satisfying)

For advanced players: feed them something harmless but ridiculous.

Suddenly, Aunt Linda thinks you've joined a medieval jousting club. Enjoy the chaos.

5. Protect Your Inner Circle

Share your real business only with people who have proven they can keep it.

If you can't think of anyone? Congratulations, you've identified the problem.

Bottom Line

You can't stop the family gossip machine, but you *can* stop being the headline. The less you give them to work with, the more they have to invent, and honestly, their fiction is often more entertaining than the truth.

Chapter 43:
Being the Truth Teller in a Family That Loves Lies

Some families thrive on love. Others thrive on lies, half-truths, and a suspicious amount of "I don't recall that happening."

If you're the truth teller, you've probably been called "dramatic," "too sensitive," or my personal favourite, "the problem."

Spoiler: you're not the problem, you're the mirror, and they don't like what they see.

1. Understand the Ecosystem

In a lie-loving family, every member has a role:

- **The Story Spinner** – Can turn "I'm tired" into "She's in rehab" by lunch.

- **The Pretender** – Smiles sweetly in public, wreaks havoc in private.
- **The Enabler** – Knows the truth, stays silent to keep the peace.
- **The Truth Teller** – That's you… Poor, sweet you.

2. Know the Risk

Telling the truth in a family allergic to it is like waving raw steak at a hungry tiger; you will be attacked.

Prepare for:

- The *"You're making things up"* defence.
- Selective amnesia.
- Suddenly being uninvited to group events.

3. Pick Your Moments

Not every hill is worth dying on.

Ask yourself:

- *Will telling this truth change anything?*
- *Is this for me, or is it for them?*

Sometimes silence protects your peace more than the truth ever will. Other times, you have to let it fly because living in lies makes you itch.

4. Don't Expect Applause

There will be no thank-you parade for "clearing the air."

In fact, the air will become thicker, frostier, and filled with muttered comments about "how you always stir things up."

5. Protect Your Energy

The truth doesn't need defending every second of the day. It's not your job to correct every lie at the dinner table.

Choose your battles, then go home and vent to a friend who *gets it*.

Bottom Line

Being the truth teller in a family that loves lies isn't about fixing them; it's about not losing yourself in their make-believe.

They might rewrite history, but you're allowed to live in the real version.

Chapter 44:
How to Survive the Golden Child Syndrome (When You're Not It)

Every family seems to have one. The chosen one. The untouchable. The golden child who could set the house on fire and be applauded for "showing initiative."

Meanwhile, you could cure a disease, and they'd ask why you didn't do it sooner.

1. Understand the Golden Child Economy

In this system, **praise is currency**, and it's all going to them.

- They can do no wrong.
- You can do no right.

- Any success you have? "That's nice, but have you seen what *they* did?"

It's not about fairness. It's about the family maintaining their favourite, even if it's completely irrational.

2. Stop Competing in a Rigged Game

You will not win. The scoreboard is fixed.

If you chase their approval, you'll spend your life overachieving and still feeling like you came second in a race you trained for your whole life.

3. See the Reality, Not the Pedestal

Golden Child Syndrome isn't actually a blessing for them either; it comes with its own poison. They're under constant pressure to stay perfect, and sometimes they're so used to special treatment they can't form healthy adult relationships.

This doesn't excuse their bad behaviour, but it does mean you don't need to envy the role.

4. Build a Life Outside the Comparison Game

Your worth is not a family scoreboard. Find people who see *you*, not the family's favourite.

Pour your energy into relationships, work, and hobbies that have nothing to do with your family's pecking order.

5. Protect Your Peace

Limit situations that make you feel invisible. If every family event turns into "The Golden

Child Show," consider shorter visits or even skipping some entirely.

Bottom Line:

The Golden Child role is a family-made crown, but it's also a cage. You don't need to wear either.

Chapter 45:
The Art of the Strategic Disinvite

There's an art to keeping your peace, and sometimes that art involves **keeping certain people far, far away from your events.**

The problem? In families, removing someone from a guest list can feel like detonating a social grenade. But it can be done, gracefully, tactfully, and without setting off Aunt Linda's Facebook rant.

1. Decide If the Disinvite Is Worth It

Ask yourself:

- Is this about protecting *me* or just avoiding discomfort?
- Will their presence ruin the event?
- Have they shown consistent disrespect?

If the answer is "yes" to more than one of these, it's not pettiness — it's self-preservation.

2. Use the Pre-Event "Boundary Buffer"

Instead of a blunt "You're not invited," you use strategic wording:

"This year we're keeping it small/low-key."
"We've had to limit the guest list."

This works best when paired with **zero extra details**. The more you explain, the more ammo they have to argue.

3. Control the Narrative Before They Do

If you know they'll try to make you the villain, tell your side *once* to the people who matter, not to the whole group chat. Overexplaining just drags you into drama.

4. Don't Break Your Own Rule

If you tell them, "We're keeping it to immediate family," don't then invite your best friend, neighbour, and Pilates instructor. Nothing blows up a boundary faster than your own inconsistency.

5. Prepare for the Fallout

Yes, some people will be mad. That's not your problem. Their reaction is proof the disinvite was probably the right choice.

Bottom Line:

The strategic disinvite isn't about being petty, it's about creating an event where you can breathe, relax, and actually enjoy yourself without scanning the room for emotional landmines.

Chapter 46:
The Emotional Cost
of the "Peacemaker" Role

Every family has one.

The *Peacemaker*.

The person who smooths over arguments, keeps everyone civil at holidays, and tries to make sure nobody storms off in the middle of dessert.

If you're reading this, it's probably you.

And I hate to break it to you, but the role is exhausting, thankless, and not actually fixing anything.

1. The Myth of the "Good Daughter/Sibling"

From the outside, the peacemaker role looks noble. Inside? It's a slow drain on your mental health. You're the one sacrificing your own comfort so *everyone else* can be comfortable — even if they're the ones causing the chaos.

2. Why It's So Hard to Quit

- **Fear of conflict** – you've been trained to believe arguments = disaster.
- **Identity trap** – you've been "the calm one" for so long, you don't know who you are without the role.
- **Family conditioning** – you learned early that keeping the peace got you love, approval, or safety.

3. The Hidden Costs

- Burnout that feels like a permanent hangover

- Constant anxiety before any family gathering
- Emotional whiplash from playing mediator between people who *don't actually want peace*
- Being blamed when peace *doesn't* happen

4. How to Step Down Without Starting World War III

You can't just announce, "I retire." You have to **replace action with absence**.

- Don't jump into smooth arguments, sit back and let awkward silences live.
- Stop explaining one person's behaviour to another ("She didn't mean it" is banned).
- Keep your answers short and neutral when drama invites itself into your texts.

5. The Magic of Letting People Be Uncomfortable

If Uncle Frank and Aunt Susan want to bicker over the potato salad, let them.

It's not your job to referee grown adults. Your only job is to protect your energy.

Bottom Line:

The family peacemaker isn't the hero; they're the unpaid, emotionally exhausted event staff. When you step back, you give yourself the freedom to enjoy family moments without running crisis control in the background.

Chapter 47: Why Going No Contact Is Sometimes the Healthiest Move

If you've ever considered cutting off a family member and immediately felt guilty… congratulations, you've been successfully trained to believe blood automatically equals loyalty.

Here's the truth:

You can love someone from a distance, even if that distance is permanent.

1. The Real Reasons People Go No Contact

It's not because you're dramatic, cold, or holding grudges. It's because:

- Every interaction leaves you drained, anxious, or in tears
- They don't respect your boundaries
- They've made zero effort to change toxic behaviour, even after multiple conversations
- Your physical or emotional safety is at risk

2. The Lies People Will Tell You About It

- "Family is everything." (Not when 'everything' means constant chaos.)
- "You'll regret it when they're gone." (You regret every time they were *here* and harmful.)
- "You're overreacting." (Said by people who benefit from your silence.)

3. How to Do It Without the Extra Trauma

- **Decide quietly**, you don't need a dramatic announcement
- **Set a clean boundary** — no half-in, half-out

- **Block or mute** — you can't heal if the door's left cracked open for guilt texts
- **Tell only safe people** — avoid explaining yourself to those who'll try to talk you out of it

4. Dealing With the Fallout

People will *talk*. They'll call you selfish, heartless, even unstable. That's because your absence makes them uncomfortable; it forces them to look at the truth you walked away from.

Remember: other people's discomfort is not your emergency.

5. Life After No Contact

Once you remove the constant drip of stress, your nervous system will thank you. You'll sleep better. Laugh more. Breathe deeper.

You'll realise how much energy you were spending trying to keep a broken relationship alive, and what you can finally do with that energy instead.

Bottom Line:

No contact isn't a punishment; it's a boundary with teeth. You're not shutting someone out for fun; you're shutting them out to survive. And survival, my dear, is never something to apologise for.

Chapter 48: How to Set Boundaries with Parents Without Feeling Like a Monster

Parents are often the hardest people to set boundaries with.

Not because you *can't*, but because it can feel like you're breaking some unwritten law that says "thou shalt forever be available to thy mother and father at all times, regardless of emotional cost."

Spoiler: that's not a law. That's conditioning.

1. Understand the Guilt Trap

When you tell a parent, "I can't do that", and they respond with:

- "After everything I've done for you?"

- "I guess I'm just a terrible parent then."
- "Fine, don't worry about me. I'll be *fine*."

That's not love. That's emotional manipulation with a parental bow on top.

2. Decide Your Boundaries Before You Need Them

If you wait until you're in the moment, guilt and old habits will take over.

Figure out now:

- How often do you want to see or speak to them
- What topics are off-limits
- What behaviour will make you leave a conversation or visit

3. Use the "Kind But Firm" Formula

Boundaries don't have to be explosive. Try:

"I love you, but I'm not willing to talk about [topic]. Let's focus on something else."
"I can visit for two hours on Sunday, but I won't be staying overnight."
"I'm not comfortable with that, so I'll pass."

Short. Clear. No apology attached.

4. Expect Pushback (and Don't Take It Personally)

When you set a boundary, you're essentially saying, "The rules have changed."

If they're used to you having none, they *will* resist.

Their reaction isn't proof you're wrong; it's proof the boundary is needed.

5. The Monster Myth

Parents who can't separate their needs from your life will sometimes make you feel like the villain for protecting your peace.

You are not abandoning them. You are not disrespecting them.

You are teaching them how to treat you — even if they never learn.

Bottom Line:

Boundaries with parents are not acts of cruelty. They are the scaffolding that holds up your emotional health. And sometimes, the most loving thing you can do for yourself (and the relationship) is to put that scaffolding in place and keep it there.

Chapter 49:
The Auntie Who Turns Every Conversation into a Roast

Some aunts knit.

Some aunts bake.

And then there's *your* aunt, who apparently moonlights as a roast comic in the secret family comedy club no one else has tickets to.

She greets you with a smile that says, "Hi sweetie," but a tone that says, "Sit down, you're about to be served."

1. Recognise It for What It Is

It's not *banter* if it leaves you feeling small.

It's not *teasing* if it's the same tired joke about your weight, job, relationship status, or that one haircut mistake you made in 2007.

It's low-effort cruelty dressed up as entertainment.

2. Decide How You'll Respond Before the Family BBQ

You have options:

- **The Stone Wall:** Smile blandly and change the subject. ("Anyway, did you see the potato salad?")
- **The Mirror:** Repeat her joke back word-for-word with a puzzled look. Sometimes hearing herself kills the punchline.
- **The Boundary Bomb:** "That's not funny to me. Please stop."
- **The Comic Upgrade:** Hit her with a joke so sharp it makes her blink and remember you're not the punching bag.

3. The Art of the Pivot

A master move is the **pivot roast redirect**:

Auntie: "Still single? Better freeze those eggs!"
You: "Speaking of things that need freezing, how's your fridge holding up? Heard it's older than the family drama."

You've shifted the target *without* getting nasty, and now the room's laughing *with* you, not at you.

4. Limit the Stage Time

If Auntie's roasts always come out after her second glass of wine or halfway through the turkey carving, that's your cue to disappear.

Kitchen help? Sure. Bathroom break? Absolutely.

Strategic retreat is a boundary in motion.

5. Don't Mistake Volume for Validity

Some relatives think that being loud, confident, and quick with insults makes them the authority on everything.

They're not. They're just *loud*.

Volume doesn't make them right, and silence doesn't make you weak.

Bottom Line:

Whether you clap back or walk away, the goal is the same: protect your peace and remind Auntie that you're not the opening act in her roast night.

Chapter 50: When Siblings Become Strangers

Once upon a time, you couldn't imagine a life where you weren't in each other's pockets, sharing snacks, secrets, and the occasional mutual cover-up of something you definitely weren't supposed to do.

Then somewhere along the line, the bond thinned.

Maybe it was slow, maybe it was sudden, but now you speak less like siblings and more like polite acquaintances.

1. Accept the Reality Before You Try to Change It

It's easy to get stuck in *"But they're my brother/sister, we're supposed to be close!"*

But relationships, even family, aren't immune to drift.

Closeness isn't a permanent setting; it's a connection you both have to maintain.

2. Stop Grieving the Fantasy Version

You're not losing *the sibling you have now*; you're grieving *the sibling they used to be*.

That version may never come back. And while that's painful, accepting it frees you from chasing a ghost.

3. Define What You Want (and What You Don't)

Do you want to rebuild the closeness?

Or do you just want a civil, drama-free connection at family gatherings?

Clarity here protects you from pouring emotional energy into someone who isn't willing to meet you halfway.

4. Reduce the Transactional Pressure

When a relationship is already strained, avoid making every interaction about solving "the problem."

Sometimes just sending a random "Saw this and thought of you" text, or tagging them in something funny, can thaw the ice without forcing an emotional deep dive.

5. When It's Time to Let Go

If your sibling becomes hostile, manipulative, or openly disrespectful, it's okay to step back.

You're not required to put yourself in emotional harm's way just because you share DNA.

Family ties are not a free pass for bad behaviour.

6. Building Peace Without the Picture-Perfect Ending

The healthiest ending isn't always reconciliation; sometimes it's accepting distance without bitterness.

You can honour the good memories without letting the bad moments define you.

Bottom Line:

Siblings aren't always forever in the way we imagine.

If the connection is salvageable, nurture it.

If it's not, release it, because the family you build for yourself matters just as much as the one you were born into.

Chapter 51:
How to Handle In-Laws Without Losing Your Sanity

Marrying someone doesn't just give you a spouse; it's like signing an *unspoken* contract that you'll now be sharing holidays, group texts, and unsolicited opinions with a brand-new set of people.

And some in-laws are wonderful, warm, welcoming, and capable of making you feel like you've known them forever.

Others... make you Google "fake your own death" before Thanksgiving.

1. Remember: They're Your Partner's People, Not Your Project

Your job isn't to fix them, win them over, or explain every choice you make.

Your only role is to keep interactions respectful and maintain your own peace.

This isn't a reality show; you don't have to win "Fan Favourite."

2. Establish the No-Go Zones Early

If they love to give unsolicited parenting advice, diet commentary, or "helpful" critiques of your life choices, draw the line politely but firmly.

For example:

"We do things a little differently in our house, but I appreciate your input."
Repeat as necessary. Eventually, they'll get bored and move on to judging someone else.

3. Keep Your Partner in the Loop

If something crosses the line, talk to your spouse privately, not in front of the whole family.

The goal isn't to start a battle, it's to get on the same team.

When they defend you in the moment, it sends a loud message without a single raised voice.

4. The Art of the Strategic Exit

Whether it's a toxic conversation or a holiday gathering that's gone nuclear, have a pre-planned "out" signal with your partner.

It can be as simple as, *"We've got that early morning thing tomorrow, we'd better head off."*

Yes, that "early morning thing" is just sleeping in your own bed in peace.

5. Don't Take the Bait

Some in-laws test boundaries just to see how you'll react.

When you refuse to engage in the drama, you take away their power.

Picture yourself behind a velvet rope. Not everyone gets access.

6. Protect Your Own Holidays

You are not contractually obligated to attend every event, every year, for the rest of your life.

Sometimes the healthiest thing you can do is alternate holidays, host your own traditions, or skip the chaos entirely.

Bottom Line:

In-laws can be an extension of your family or a constant stress test.

Your job isn't to pass with perfect scores, it's to protect your sanity, keep your partnership strong, and never let someone else's bad behaviour make you feel small in your own life.

Chapter 52: Why Family Group Chats Are Emotional Minefields

On paper, family group chats sound harmless. A nice little space for quick updates, photos of the kids, and holiday planning.

In reality? It's a digital Wild West where boundaries go to die.

1. The 6 Types of Group Chat Landmines

The Oversharer

They post every detail of their medical procedures, complete with blurry hospital selfies.

The Guilt Tripper

Drops a passive-aggressive "Guess no one wants to talk to me" if no one replies in 30 seconds.

The Troll

Purposely starts political debates at 9:47pm on a Tuesday.

The Rival Parent

Uploads every achievement of their child, followed by, *"What's little Timmy up to these days?"* with a smug smile emoji.

The Ghost

Never participates but mysteriously pops up to comment when gossip is involved.

The Chain Messenger

Still sends "Forward this or your crush will never love you" in 2025.

2. How to Survive Without Throwing Your Phone

Mute the Thread

The first rule of family chat survival: the mute button is your best friend.

You can dip in when you have the energy and avoid being sucked into a 47-message back-and-forth about potato salad recipes.

Use the "Like" Button Liberally

No energy for a full reply? Tap the thumbs-up and move on. Instant participation with minimal effort.

Avoid the 'Danger Words'

Some topics are a one-way ticket to chaos. Politics, parenting, religion, and "Who's hosting Christmas?" — tread carefully.

3. Boundaries Apply Here Too

You can leave a group chat.

Yes, there will be drama, but sometimes it's worth the freedom.

Just screenshot any important info before you go, and then *walk away slowly, without looking back.*

4. Reframe the Purpose

If you can't leave, redefine it in your mind: it's not a sacred space, it's background noise.

Like the radio in a shop, it's on, but you don't have to dance to every song.

Bottom Line:

Family group chats aren't inherently evil, but they're fertile ground for misunderstandings, passive aggression, and subtle manipulation.

The key is to participate on *your* terms, not out of obligation, and not at the expense of your mental health.

Chapter 53: The Uncle Who Drinks and Thinks He's Wise

Every family has *that* uncle. The one who clinks his glass, clears his throat, and suddenly everyone's trapped in a 45-minute speech about "how the world really works."

He's part philosopher, part conspiracy theorist, and part walking cautionary tale. The problem? He's absolutely convinced his alcohol-soaked life lessons are universal truths.

1. The Greatest Hits of Drunken Wisdom

The "Back in My Day" Lecture

Usually starts with, *"You kids don't know how good you've got it…"* and ends with you wondering how a story about the price of bread in 1973 turned into a rant about cryptocurrency.

The Political Monologue

No matter the occasion, Christmas lunch, your cousin's baby shower, he'll find a way to wedge in his opinion on the government, immigration, and why "nobody works hard anymore."

The Wild Life Advice

Often contradicts itself.

Example: *"Never trust anyone."* Two minutes later: *"You gotta believe in people."*

2. Survival Strategies for His Speeches

Adopt the Goldfish Attention Span

Smile, nod, and let your mind wander. Think about dinner. Think about puppies. Think about anything but what he's saying.

Tag-Team Escapes

Develop a secret rescue signal with another family member, a subtle eyebrow raise that means *"Save me now."*

The Bathroom Break Tactic

Nobody questions it. Works every time. Bonus points if you take your drink with you so you can "top it up."

3. What Not to Do

- **Do not** argue, he's immune to facts after drink number three.
- **Do not** try to match his energy; you'll lose and possibly end up in your own embarrassing family story.

- **Do not** encourage him with *"Tell us more"* unless you have nowhere to be for the next three hours.

4. Finding the Funny Side

If all else fails, treat it like a free comedy show. Collect his wildest quotes and save them for your group chat with friends.

My personal favourite?

"You can't trust banks… but you should open one."

Bottom Line:

Uncle Wisdom isn't going to change, but you can change how much of your time and energy you give him.

Keep your boundaries firm, your exits planned, and your sense of humour intact.

Chapter 54: Navigating Funerals Without Digging Emotional Graves

Funerals are supposed to be about paying respects and honouring the life of someone who's passed. Unfortunately, they're also like a high-stakes family reunion where decades of unresolved drama gather in one awkwardly silent room.

If weddings bring out the best in people, funerals bring out the *truth*. And sometimes, the truth is… your family is one snide remark away from re-enacting a soap opera scene in front of the casket.

1. The Social Olympics of Funerals

The Long-Lost Relative with Selective Memory

They haven't spoken to you in twenty years, but now they're acting like you shared a bunk bed and secrets every night growing up.

The Competitive Mourner

Crying louder, hugging longer, sighing heavier, determined to prove they loved the deceased *most*.

The Blame-Thrower

Subtly (or not so subtly) implying *someone* should've done more to prevent this. Spoiler: it's usually aimed at whoever organised the funeral.

2. Survival Rules for the Day

Rule #1: Pick Your Seat Wisely

Avoid sitting next to people who might whisper criticisms mid-service. You're here to mourn, not host *Mystery Science Funeral 3000*.

Rule #2: Limit Your Conversations

Stick to safe topics like the weather, how nice the flowers look, or "they really would've loved this song." Don't take the bait on anything deeper.

Rule #3: Perfect the Polite Exit

If someone starts venting about a family feud, excuse yourself to "check on the catering", even if there isn't any.

3. The Eulogy Minefield

If you're asked to speak, remember:

- This is not your chance to air grievances.
- Keep it under five minutes; this is a eulogy, not a podcast.
- If you can't say something nice, stick to universally safe lines like *"They loved their garden"* or *"They were truly one of a kind."*

4. Why Funerals Can Reopen Old Wounds

Grief has a way of unearthing more than memories. It brings old hurts, rivalries, and unspoken resentments to the surface.

The trick is to remember, this day is not about fixing the family. It's about honouring the person you've lost, in your own way, without adding to the emotional casualty count.

Bottom Line:

Funerals are hard enough without the added pressure of navigating family landmines. Be kind, be brief, and don't let anyone bait you into an argument. The goal is to leave with your dignity and your peace intact.

Chapter 55:
The Cousin Who Competes Like It's the Olympics

Every family has *that* cousin.

The one who treats every gathering like an opportunity to rack up imaginary medals in the sport of "Being Better Than You."

It doesn't matter what the event is, a baby shower, a barbecue, or Nan's 80th, somehow, they manage to turn it into a full-blown competition. And of course, they're winning. In their head.

1. Events in the Family Games

The "Look What I Bought" Relay

They'll find a way to mention their new car, designer handbag, or just how "exclusive" their holiday destination was, even if the topic was originally about your cat's dental surgery.

The "Better Parent" Gymnastics

If you have kids, they have kids who sleep better, eat cleaner, and excel at *every* sport. If you don't have kids, their children are still somehow outperforming you.

The Income High Jump

Somehow, you always find yourself trapped in a casual conversation that magically morphs into a breakdown of their salary, investment portfolio, or "side hustle" that's *just exploded lately*.

2. How to Spot Them Quickly

- They enter the room with the same energy as an athlete at the opening ceremony.

- Within five minutes, you know their current job title, gym routine, and the exact price of their latest purchase.
- You leave the conversation feeling like you just lost a game you didn't even know you were playing.

3. Strategies to Keep Your Sanity

Option 1: Play the Diplomatic Spectator

Smile, nod, and say "That's great!" like you're a sports commentator. Don't engage, don't compare, don't give them more fuel.

Option 2: Change the Event Mid-Game

"Oh, speaking of your new car, did you hear about Uncle Ray's goat getting loose in the post office?" Distract and redirect.

Option 3: Keep Your Own Score

Every time they humblebrag, mentally award yourself points for *not* caring. Bonus points if you can escape the conversation in under three minutes.

4. Why They Do It

The competitive cousin is usually driven by insecurity dressed as confidence. Their bragging isn't really about you; it's about convincing themselves they're doing okay.

Bottom Line:

You can't stop them from competing, but you *can* stop signing up for their events. The less you play, the less power they have, and the sooner you can get back to actually enjoying your family time.

Chapter 56:
How to Spot Financial Manipulation in Family

Money and family are a dangerous mix. Add in a little manipulation, and suddenly you're not lending $50, you're "investing in a shared dream" that you didn't agree to and will never see again.

Financial manipulation in families doesn't always look like outright theft. Sometimes, it's coated in guilt, wrapped in obligation, and served with a side of "But we're family…"

1. Classic Signs of Financial Manipulation

The "Guilt Loan"

They remind you of everything they've *ever* done for you before asking for money. Bonus points if they bring up a childhood story you barely remember.

The "Silent Invoice"

They do you a small favour, and then act like you now owe them something huge, forever.

The "Emergency That Isn't"

A sudden crisis that must be fixed *right now*, usually involving rent, bills, or "unexpected expenses." Later, you find out the money went to a new phone or a weekend away.

The "Group Project" Trap

They pitch a family investment opportunity that "we'll all benefit from," but somehow you're the only one actually putting in cash.

2. How They Keep You Hooked

- **Emotional Blackmail**: "If you really cared, you'd help."
- **Public Pressure**: Asking in front of other relatives so saying "no" makes you look bad.
- **Shifting Goalposts**: You agree to one thing, and suddenly the amount or terms change.

3. How to Protect Yourself

Set Your Money Boundary in Stone

Have a rule — maybe it's "I don't lend to family" or "I only give what I can afford to never get back." Stick to it, no exceptions.

Ask for Details (Without Apology)

If they're vague about why they need the money, that's a red flag. If they can't give you specifics, don't give them cash.

Redirect Instead of Handing Over Cash

Offer to pay the bill directly, buy the groceries, or help them find other resources. This stops the "oops, I spent it on something else" problem.

Be Okay with the Discomfort

Saying "no" may make you feel like the bad guy, but it's better than resenting them forever.

Bottom Line:

Family or not, you are not an ATM. Your financial stability matters too and protecting it doesn't make you selfish; it makes you smart.

Chapter 57: Breaking the Cycle of Family Guilt Trips

Guilt is one of the oldest tools in the toxic family toolbox. It's sneaky, it's effective, and it works because it targets your soft spots, your love for them, your sense of duty, and that little voice in your head that whispers *"Maybe they're right…"*.

The truth? Guilt trips are emotional manipulation disguised as concern, tradition, or morality. And once you learn to spot them, you can finally get off the ride.

1. How to Recognise a Guilt Trip in Progress

The History Weapon

They bring up something they did for you years ago, as if your entire life is now a repayment plan.

The 'Good Child' Card

"You're the only one in the family who can be trusted to do this." Translation: *We know you're too nice to say no.*

The Bad Reputation Threat

"If you don't help, everyone will think you've changed." Spoiler: that's called growth.

The Family Reputation Shield

They frame it as protecting the family name, when really, it's about avoiding their own discomfort.

2. Why Guilt Trips Work So Well

- You've been trained from a young age to put their needs first.
- Saying "no" feels like rejecting the person, not just the request.
- The discomfort is immediate, while the benefits of setting boundaries take longer to feel.

3. How to Break the Cycle

Call It Out (Calmly)

You don't have to start a fight, but you can name what's happening:

"That sounds like a guilt trip, and I'm not comfortable making decisions that way."

Separate the Request from the Relationship

Just because you say "no" to the request doesn't mean you're saying "no" to the relationship.

Don't Over-Explain

The more reasons you give, the more ammo they have to argue back. A simple "That doesn't work for me" is enough.

Accept That They Might Be Upset

Your job isn't to manage their feelings, it's to protect your well-being.

Bottom Line:

Breaking the cycle of family guilt trips takes practice, but every time you hold your ground, you teach them (and yourself) that your boundaries aren't negotiable.

Chapter 58: Why You're Not Obligated to Play Host for Toxic People

Some families think "hosting" is an honour.

But when the guest list includes people who make you tense, exhausted, or emotionally wrecked, it's not an honour, it's an unpaid endurance event.

1. The Myth of the Good Host

We've been fed the idea that a "good" person never turns away family, no matter how they behave. But hospitality isn't about sacrificing your peace to keep someone else comfortable.

You're not a hotel. You're not an emotional Airbnb. You're a human being with limits.

2. Signs You Shouldn't Host Them

- You spend more time cleaning, cooking, and preparing than actually enjoying your own home.
- You find yourself rehearsing comebacks for their predictable passive-aggressive comments.
- You need a week to recover after they leave.
- Your children, pets, or partner tense up when they walk through the door.

3. How to Say No Without Burning the House Down

Offer Neutral Ground

Instead of "Come over," try, "Let's catch up at a café."

Blame the Space

"My place is too small for hosting right now." (*Translation: too small for your energy.*)

Set a Time Limit

If you must host, keep it short: "We'd love to see you for an hour in the afternoon."

Make It Seasonal

"We've decided to host just once a year, and we've already had our gathering."

4. The Emotional Payoff

When you stop opening your home to toxic people, you:

- Protect your mental space.
- Stop dreading visits.
- Send the message that your home is a safe zone, not a battleground.

Bottom Line:

Hosting is a privilege, not an obligation. The right guests fill your home with warmth. The wrong ones fill it with stress, and stress doesn't deserve a spare room.

Chapter 59:
The Myth of
"Blood Is Thicker Than Water"

We've all heard it, usually from someone who just treated us poorly and still expects a Christmas invite:

"But… we're family."

It's meant to be the ultimate guilt-trip. The unshakable reason why you must forgive, forget, and put up with anything. But here's the truth: the full phrase isn't what you think it is.

1. The Original Saying Got Lost in Translation

The actual old proverb was closer to:

"The blood of the covenant is thicker than the water of the womb."

Which means, the relationships you choose (your "covenant") can be stronger than the ones you're born into.

Somewhere along the way, society chopped it up and spun it into a loyalty clause for people who hadn't earned it.

2. Why This Myth is Dangerous

- **It excuses bad behaviour** — as if sharing DNA is a free pass for cruelty.
- **It traps people in cycles of abuse** because "family always comes first."
- **It invalidates chosen family** — the friends and partners who've shown up for you more than relatives ever have.

3. What Actually Makes a Relationship Strong

It's not blood.

It's trust. Respect. Effort.

It's being there when it matters.

It's treating someone with kindness even when no one is watching.

4. How to Reframe This in Your Life

- Remind yourself: **Connection is about choice, not obligation.**
- Value the people who've earned their place in your life.
- Stop using family titles as shields for bad behaviour.
- Give yourself permission to step back from relatives who hurt you.

5. The Freedom of Letting Go

Once you stop clinging to the "blood is thicker" myth, you realise you're allowed to:

- Keep boundaries high.
- Spend holidays with people you actually like.
- Build a life where love is given freely, not demanded.

Bottom Line:

Family is not a get-out-of-accountability-free card.

Sometimes the strongest bonds are the ones we create, not the ones we inherit.

Chapter 60: How to Build Your Own Chosen Family

Some people are born into love.

Others have to go out and **find** it, brick by brick, like building a house from scratch.

If your birth family feels more like a hostile work environment than a safe haven, you're not broken; you're just in the wrong team. And the best news? You can draft your own players.

1. What is a Chosen Family?

It's the people you deliberately welcome into your life who:

- Celebrate your wins without jealousy
- Stand by you in your lowest moments

- Respect your boundaries without sulking
- Make your life feel lighter, not heavier

They don't need to share your DNA to feel like home.

2. Finding the Right People

A. Start with Your Interests

Join spaces where people share your passions, hobby groups, classes, online communities. Shared joy is a fast bond.

B. Notice Who Feels Safe

Pay attention to the people who don't drain you, who listen without judgement, and who never use your vulnerabilities against you.

C. Take It Slow

A chosen family is built over time, not in a weekend. Real trust grows layer by layer.

3. The Ground Rules for Your New Family

- **No silent treatments as punishment**
- **Respect for boundaries** is non-negotiable
- **Mutual effort**, it's not a one-way street
- **Conflict is addressed, not buried**

4. Why This Matters for Neurodivergent Women

If you're neurodivergent, you may have been told since childhood to mask your needs or accept mistreatment to "keep the peace."

A chosen family allows you to be your unfiltered self without fear of losing love.

5. Nurturing Your New Circle

- Create traditions that are yours, from Sunday brunch to group trips
- Celebrate milestones, big or small
- Protect the space from toxic influences, even if that means cutting off old connections

Bottom Line:

You don't have to keep showing up for people who keep letting you down. Love is not about obligation, it's about choice. And the family you choose can be the one that finally gives you the peace, laughter, and safety you've always deserved.

ACT 3 – The Rise

Healing, boundaries, and becoming impossible to walk over.

Chapter 61:
How to Rebuild When You're Starting from Zero

There's a strange kind of freedom in having nothing left.

When the people who drained you have finally drifted out of orbit, when the noise dies down, when your phone is quieter than a library at midnight... It's just you.

No more performances. No more placating. No more explaining.

It's terrifying.

It's liberating.

And if you let it, it's the beginning of everything.

You are not rebuilding who you were before, she didn't survive this far by accident, but she also didn't know what you know now.

You are building *new*.

From the ground up.

From the ashes, yes, but this time you get to choose the shape of the phoenix.

Here's where you start:

- **Clear the rubble** – delete the numbers, unfollow the feeds, throw out the half-broken reminders of people who broke you. Make room before you make plans.
- **Choose your bricks**, every boundary, every self-care habit, every "no" you say is a brick in the foundation of your new life.
- **Stop asking for permission** – no one else gets a vote in what your rebuild looks like.
- **Think long-term joy, not quick comfort** – you're not patching a leaky roof here, you're designing a home for your soul.

Yes, you'll have moments where it feels impossible. Where the quiet feels too loud. Where you'll want to text the very people who helped knock you down, just so you don't feel alone.

But you won't.

Because you didn't come this far to trade your fresh start for a rerun of old pain.

The hardest part about starting from zero is believing that zero isn't the end.

It's the clean page, the open sky, the plot twist you write for yourself.

And this time, the story is yours.

Chapter 62:
Stop Explaining and Start Living

You don't owe anyone a PowerPoint presentation on why you're living your life the way you are.

Not your family.

Not your friends.

Not that ex who still watches your Instagram stories like it's their part-time job.

Here's the truth:

Every time you over-explain yourself, you hand someone else the pen to write your story.

You let them believe their approval is a requirement.

And guess what? It isn't.

Think about how much time and energy you've spent trying to "make them understand" in the past. Hours. Days. Whole *eras* of your life wasted in circular conversations with people who had no intention of listening in the first place.

You could have learned a language by now. Or planted a garden. Or, at the very least, finished that Netflix series you abandoned in season two.

The shift is this:

You don't need them to get it. You just need to get on with it.

That means:

- **Make decisions quietly** – and then live them loudly.
- **Stop arguing with people committed to misunderstanding you** – their confusion isn't your problem to solve.

- **Let your actions be the proof** – because when you're thriving, you won't need to explain.

And here's the magic part:

When you stop explaining and start living, you get your energy back.

You stop editing your life for the comfort of people who would never edit theirs for you.

And that's when the real growth happens, not in the approval, but in the unapologetic momentum.

The people who matter will see you.

The rest can keep guessing.

Chapter 63: Finding Your People in the Wild

Once you stop explaining yourself, you clear space for the people who just *get* you.

No subtitles. No disclaimers. No "Sorry, I'm a bit much" preface.

But here's the reality check:

Finding your people doesn't happen by scrolling aimlessly or waiting for the universe to deliver them to your doorstep like an Amazon Prime order. You have to put yourself where your kind of people actually *are*.

Step one: Know what you're looking for.

If you're craving friends who match your ambition, go where ambitious people hang out, workshops, industry events, niche online communities.

If you want soft, slow, Sunday-afternoon friends, try book clubs, art classes, or local cafes.

If you want people who understand your neurodivergent brain without judgement, join spaces where that's the norm, not the exception.

Step two: Test the energy early.

Look for signs of acceptance without performance. Do they light up when you share your weird? Or do they go quiet, make a joke, or change the subject? The right people won't make you feel like a cautionary tale.

Step three: Choose depth over volume.

Five genuine connections beat fifty shallow ones every time. These are the people who will answer your call when you're at rock bottom and scream with joy when you're on the way up.

And here's the thing, your people are probably also out there searching for you.

So be findable. Share your passions, your humour, your quirks. Don't dim them in the name of fitting in.

When you find your people in the wild, it's not just friendship.

It's a homecoming you didn't even know you were missing.

Chapter 64: The 90-Day Boundary Reset

Boundaries aren't just about saying *no*, they're about teaching people how to treat you and teaching *yourself* that your time, energy, and peace matter.

But here's the problem: if you've gone years without boundaries, your life can look like a crowded house party where everyone's inside, drinking your drinks, eating your snacks, and leaving their shoes on your couch.

You don't just throw them all out at once; you clear the room in a way that sticks.

That's where the **90-Day Boundary Reset** comes in.

Month 1: Declutter

- **Audit your life.** Who drains you? Who respects you? Make three lists: "Keep," "Reassess," and "Exit."
- **Pause automatic yeses.** When someone asks for your time or energy, say, "Let me check and get back to you."
- **Reduce overexposure.** Limit how often you see or speak to the biggest boundary-breakers.

Month 2: Define

- **Get specific.** A boundary like "I need space" is vague. Try, "I'm not available for calls after 8 PM" or "I don't discuss my dating life with family."
- **Practice micro-boundaries.** Small acts of self-protection, like muting chats, turning off read receipts, or setting meeting limits.
- **Communicate once.** Boundaries aren't an endless debate. You state them clearly, kindly, and then you enforce them.

Month 3: Defend

- **Hold the line.** Expect pushback. People who benefitted from your lack of boundaries will test the new ones.
- **Refuse guilt bait.** "You've changed" is often code for "I can't use you like before."
- **Reward yourself.** Boundaries are hard work, especially if you've been a chronic people-pleaser. Celebrate every win.

At the end of 90 days, you'll notice something.

Your stress is lower. Your calendar is lighter. Your relationships are more intentional. And the people who remain? They're there because they want *you*, not what they can get from you.

A boundary reset isn't about building walls.

It's about building a life where only the right people get a key.

Chapter 65: Relearning Trust Without Losing Your Guard

When you've been lied to, betrayed, or drained for sport, trusting again can feel like asking a paper cut to swim in lemon juice.

You know you can't live in total isolation forever, but the thought of opening the door, even a crack, feels like an invitation to another disaster.

The goal isn't to drop your guard completely.

The goal is to let *good* people in while keeping the wrong ones out.

Step 1: Redefine What Trust Means

For years, you may have equated trust with *blind faith*. That's not trust, that's gambling.

Real trust is built in **layers**, consistent actions over time. No fast passes, no shortcuts.

Step 2: Start with Low Stakes

Don't hand over your deepest secrets on the first coffee date.

Start with small opportunities for trust:

- Share a minor personal story and see if it stays private.
- Ask for a small favour and see if it's delivered without resentment.
- Watch how they treat service staff — it says more than any Instagram bio.

Step 3: Watch the Follow-Through

Trust isn't about *what they say*, it's about *what they repeat*.

Someone can show up once and fool you.

It's the pattern that counts.

Step 4: Keep Your Self-Trust First

The strongest shield you have is believing in your own ability to walk away.

When you know you can leave at the first red flag, it's easier to risk letting someone in, because you know you won't ignore the warning signs again.

Step 5: Accept That Fear Won't Disappear

You can rebuild trust and still feel nervous.

Caution doesn't mean you're broken; it means you've learned.

Trusting again isn't about becoming wide open.

It's about learning to open the right doors, at the right time, to the right people, and keeping the spare key for yourself.

Chapter 66:
Why Self-Respect Feels Lonely at First

No one tells you that choosing yourself can feel like the world just unfollowed you.

When you finally stop chasing people, stop saying yes out of fear, and stop tolerating crumbs, the noise in your life dies down fast.

Sometimes, it's so quiet you can hear your own heartbeat — and not in a romantic movie way, but in an *I'm-alone-on-a-Friday-night* kind of way.

The Withdrawal Phase

Self-respect is like detoxing from a toxic drug.

For years, you've been hooked on approval, attention, and connection at any cost.

Now that you're not bending over backwards for it, you feel the absence — and it's uncomfortable.

The Social Shrink

When you set boundaries, your circle might shrink.

Some people will vanish because they can no longer get away with their old behaviour.

Others will sulk because your growth makes them look bad.

The Rebuild

This is the stage where you need to resist the urge to run back to familiar chaos just so you're not lonely.

Loneliness now is temporary.

Chaos is forever if you let it back in.

The Payoff

Self-respect has a delayed gratification period.

In the beginning, it costs you company.

In the end, it rewards you with people who value you exactly as you are, without conditions or games.

Self-respect will cost you something.

But it will never cost you *yourself*.

Chapter 67:
Saying "No"
Without the Guilt Hangover

The first time you say *no* to someone who's used to hearing *yes*, brace yourself.

They'll look at you like you've just slapped a puppy.

You'll feel the pang of guilt.

And that's when the mind games start, mostly from you… on yourself.

The Old Program

We've been conditioned to believe that "no" is rude, selfish, or unkind.

So, when we say it, the guilt alarm in our brains starts blaring.

But here's the truth: saying yes when you mean no is lying, to them and to yourself.

The Micro-Dose Method

If "no" feels too big at first, start with micro-doses:

- "I can't today."
- "That doesn't work for me."
- "I'm not available."

No elaborate excuses. No over-apologising. Just a clean, clear *no*.

The Guilt Detox

Guilt after saying no isn't a sign you've done something wrong; it's a sign you're breaking a habit.

The more you practice, the less guilt will stick.

Think of it like peeling off a price tag. Sticky at first, but smooth once it's gone.

The Flip

Remember: every time you say no to something that drains you, you're saying yes to something that builds you.

That "something" is your peace, your energy, and your self-respect.

The fastest way to get rid of a guilt hangover?

Stop drinking from other people's cups when yours is already empty.

Chapter 68: How to Keep Your Peace When They Push Back

So, you've set a boundary. You've said no.

Cue the *pushback*.

Maybe it's a guilt trip. Maybe it's sarcasm.

Maybe it's the classic *silent treatment,* the emotional toddler's way of stomping off.

The Pushback Playbook

People who benefit from your lack of boundaries will never cheer for your new ones.

Expect it. Plan for it. Don't take it personally.

1. Name the Pattern, Not the Person

Instead of reacting with "You're being manipulative!", try,

"That's not going to work for me."

You're not debating their behaviour; you're reinforcing your choice.

2. Stay in Calm Mode

They want a reaction. That's the hook.

Your job? Be *boring*.

Respond like someone who has better things to do (because you do).

3. Use the Broken Record Technique

Repeat your boundary without adding fuel:

- "I understand, but my answer is the same."
- "I hear you, but that doesn't change my decision."

Eventually, they'll realise you're not moving.

4. Remember: Silence Is a Response

Sometimes the best move is no move at all.

Not every comment, jab, or sigh deserves your energy.

The reality: keeping your peace isn't about the absence of conflict,

It's about not letting the conflict *inside* you.

If they're loud, let them be loud.

If they're offended, let them be offended.

You're not here to manage their feelings, only your own.

Chapter 69: Turning Old Wounds into Wisdom

Some people collect stamps.

Some people collect spoons.

You? You've been collecting emotional scars, and not by choice.

The good news is, scars don't have to just be reminders of pain.

They can be proof of survival, and even better, blueprints for how to avoid walking into the same fire twice.

1. Stop Calling It "Wasted Time"

That relationship, that friendship, that years-long family circus you endured, it wasn't wasted.

It was tuition for the course called *I Will Never Tolerate That Again*.

2. Identify the Lesson, Not the Pain

When you think of the wound, shift your focus.

Instead of "They betrayed me," try,

"I learned what betrayal looks like early, so I can see it coming next time.

3. Turn Pain Into a Filter

Old wounds are like a built-in alarm system.

When someone starts showing the same red flags, your system pings,

"This feels familiar, let's slow down here."

4. Teach From It

You don't have to become a life coach or write a memoir,

but when someone in your world is heading toward the same kind of trouble,

share what you've learned. Even if they don't listen, you've planted the seed.

The point:

Your old wounds don't need to be locked away like embarrassing secrets.

They can be your map, your radar, your armour.

The goal isn't to forget they happened.

The goal is to make sure they mean something.

Chapter 70:
The Art of the Soft Exit from Toxic Spaces

Not every departure needs to be a dramatic storm-out with doors slamming and "You'll regret this!" echoing behind you.

Sometimes the most powerful exits are the quiet ones, no fireworks, no announcements, just... gone.

1. Stop Giving Warnings

If you've already told them the issue three times and nothing changes, they don't need another speech.

They need your absence.

2. Become Busy (Conveniently)

Decline a few invites.

Take longer to reply.

Ease yourself out until they realise, you're not orbiting their drama anymore.

3. Remove Hooks

If they can't guilt-trip you, bait you, or drag you back into arguments,

You've already half left, even if your body's still in the room.

4. Protect Your Energy Bank

Soft exits work because they stop you from overspending your emotional energy on people who can't (or won't) change.

Instead of burning the bridge, you simply stop walking across it.

The point:

Not all goodbyes need to be loud to be final.

Sometimes, the soft exit is the ultimate power move, because it leaves no cracks for them to crawl back through.

Chapter 71: How to Love Without Losing Yourself Again

Falling in love shouldn't mean falling out of yourself.

But if you've been through enough toxic relationships, you know how easy it is to start bending, shrinking, or rewriting your own needs to fit someone else's comfort zone.

1. Keep Your Identity on the Table

Your hobbies, routines, friendships, and dreams are not "extras" to be put aside when someone new enters your life.

They're *the foundation* of who you are and if they can't fit into your life as it is, they shouldn't be in it.

2. Use the "Would I Still Do This?" Test

When you make a choice for love, ask yourself:

"Would I do this if I were single?"
If the answer is no, and it's not about growth, but about appeasing, you're in danger of erasing yourself.

3. Make Boundaries Before the Butterflies

Set non-negotiables early.

It's easier to enforce a boundary you've already declared than to scramble to create one mid-relationship.

4. Love as a Whole Person

Healthy love is two complete people walking side-by-side, not two halves trying to become whole.

Your happiness, worth, and confidence should never depend on them *showing up right*.

The point:

The best relationships make you more *you*, not less.

If they love you, they'll want you to stay the main character in your own life, not a sidekick in theirs.

Chapter 72: Becoming the Main Character of Your Own Life

Somewhere between doing what's "expected" and avoiding conflict, many women forget what it's like to actually live for themselves.

You start making choices based on who will approve, who will be upset, and how much drama you'll have to clean up afterwards.

The problem? You become a background character in your own story.

1. Rewrite Your Script

Imagine your life as a movie, you're the lead, not the best friend who only exists to hype someone else's plot.

Ask:

"If this was *my* movie, what would I choose next?"
Then do that.

2. Drop the Guilt Cameo

When you're used to people-pleasing, stepping into your own spotlight can feel selfish.

It's not.

The people who benefit from you playing small will be the first to call you selfish when you finally take up space. That's not a red flag, that's proof you're on the right track.

3. Curate Your Supporting Cast

Main characters have strong boundaries about who gets screen time.

Keep the friends who cheer for your wins without secretly resenting them.

Cut the ones who treat your joy like competition.

4. Choose Plotlines That Matter

Stop agreeing to things just because "it's what people do."

Start saying yes to the things that light you up, challenge you, and pull you toward the life you actually want.

The point:

You're not here to be a prop in someone else's drama.

You're here to write your own, live it loudly, and own every scene.

Chapter 73: Why Self-Care Isn't Always Pretty

Somewhere along the way, self-care got rebranded as spa days, pastel planners, and Instagram-worthy matcha lattes.

And while those can be lovely, the truth is… real self-care is often messy, uncomfortable, and completely unphotogenic.

1. The Unseen Side of Healing

Self-care is sitting in therapy crying your makeup off because you finally said the thing you've been avoiding for years.

It's taking your medication even when it makes you feel tired.

It's cancelling plans because you can't fake being okay today.

2. The Boring Discipline

Sometimes self-care looks like doing the laundry, paying your bills, or cooking something halfway decent instead of eating chips for dinner again.

It's not glamorous. No one's clapping for you.

But it's the groundwork for the life you're building.

3. The Relationships Audit

Real self-care might mean walking away from a relationship that still has your heart but is destroying your peace.

It might mean blocking a family member on social media so they can't passive-aggressively comment on your life anymore.

4. The Truth About the Glow-Up

The glow-up isn't just about hair, nails, and a new outfit.

It's the tired, sweaty, and sometimes ugly work you do behind the scenes so your future self can stand taller.

The point:

Self-care isn't always pretty, but it's always worth it.

And the best part? You don't need anyone else's approval to do it.

Chapter 74: The Power of Going Quiet Before You Go Loud

In a world where everyone is broadcasting every opinion, every win, every "just because" selfie…

There's power in saying nothing.

1. Quiet Doesn't Mean Weak

Going quiet is not about shrinking yourself, it's about gathering your strength where nobody can drain it.

It's choosing not to hand your next move over to people who'd rather sabotage than support.

2. The Strategic Silence

You don't have to announce your boundaries for them to be real.

You don't have to explain your healing process for it to be valid.

Sometimes the most satisfying reveal is letting your results speak for themselves, after you've already done the work in private.

3. Energy Conservation Is a Power Move

Every time you explain yourself to people who aren't listening, you spend emotional currency you could be investing in your future.

Silence keeps your resources where they belong with you.

4. The Loud Entrance

When you've been building in the quiet, the moment you finally step forward, it hits different.

Not because you've been hiding, but because you've been *preparing*.

And nothing shakes the people who underestimated you more than a quiet person who suddenly shows up… unstoppable.

The point:

You don't have to tell the world you're coming, just arrive.

Chapter 75:
How to Keep Small Wins from Feeling Small

It's easy to dismiss the tiny victories when you're chasing the big ones.

You think, *I'll celebrate when it's the big milestone.*

But here's the truth, the big milestone is nothing more than a pile of small wins stacked on top of each other.

1. Stop Waiting for "The Big Moment"

That day you got out of bed after a week of burnout?

That's a win.

The moment you didn't reply to a toxic text?

That's a win.

The first time you said "no" without over-explaining?

That's *huge*.

The small wins are proof you're moving, and movement is progress.

2. Shrink the Measuring Stick

If you only measure success by once-in-a-lifetime events, you'll spend 99% of your life feeling like you're failing.

Instead, make your success metrics realistic, daily, and human.

You don't have to climb Everest — you can climb out of bed, brush your hair, and that still counts when you're rebuilding yourself.

3. Celebrate Without Justifying

You don't need to explain to anyone why you're proud.

Post about it, write it in a journal, buy yourself the cupcake, throw on your "I won" playlist, whatever feels good.

You earned the joy.

4. The Momentum Effect

Small wins keep you moving.

They create momentum, and momentum builds confidence.

Confidence pushes you toward the bigger wins faster than shame ever will.

The point:

Your "small" win might be the exact thing that keeps you going long enough to get to the big one. Don't skip the celebration.

Chapter 76: The Beauty of Having Fewer, Deeper Connections

There's a strange kind of magic that happens when you stop trying to collect people like Instagram followers and start choosing your connections with intention.

Suddenly, the room is quieter, but the conversations are richer.

1. Quality Over Quantity Isn't Just a Pinterest Quote

A hundred people can know your name, but if none of them truly *see* you, it's just noise.

A few good people who show up when it's messy, boring, or inconvenient?

That's gold.

2. The End of the People-Pleasing Era

When you stop performing for approval, you find out who actually likes the *real* you.

Some people will leave. Let them.

The ones who stay aren't there because of what you can do for them — they're there because they value who you *are*.

3. Deeper Connections Mean Safer Spaces

When your circle is smaller, trust builds faster, and boundaries are easier to keep.

You're no longer walking on eggshells or over-explaining yourself.

You can breathe, and breathing is underrated.

4. How to Nurture the Good Ones

- **Be intentional** — schedule time for them.
- **Be honest** — vulnerability is an investment.
- **Be present**, no doomscrolling while they're talking.

The point:

Life isn't about being surrounded by the most people; it's about being surrounded by the right people.

Chapter 77: Why Validation Is an Inside Job

At some point, you have to decide you're done holding auditions for the role of "person who finally makes me feel worthy."

Because here's the truth: no one can give you permanent validation.

They can sprinkle it on you like glitter, but if you don't believe it yourself, it washes off in the first rain.

1. The Problem with Outsourcing Your Worth

When you rely on others to tell you you're good enough, you give them power over your mood, your confidence, and your choices.

And some people, knowingly or not, will use that power to keep you small.

2. Validation That Lasts Has to Come from You

- It's not a one-time pep talk in the mirror.
- It's a daily decision to believe your value is constant, not based on who likes you, loves you, or leaves you.

3. Start with Self-Recognition

Instead of waiting for applause, notice your own wins:

- Did you stick to a boundary today? That's huge.
- Did you rest without guilt? That's growth.
- Did you speak up for yourself? That's courage.

4. The Freedom of Not Needing Permission

When you validate yourself, you're free to make decisions without running them through the "Will they approve?" filter.

That's when you stop living reactively and start living intentionally.

The point:

External validation is nice, but self-validation is unshakable.

When you own your worth, no one can rent space in your head without your permission.

Chapter 78:
Learning to Celebrate Yourself Out Loud

You know that awkward thing where you downplay your own wins, so no one thinks you're "full of yourself"?

Yeah, we're not doing that anymore.

1. Stop Hiding Your Happiness

Somewhere along the way, you were taught that celebrating yourself makes you arrogant, that your joy might make someone else feel small.

But here's the truth: people who are secure in themselves will clap louder, not quieter, when you win.

2. Why Celebration Matters

When you acknowledge your achievements out loud, you train your brain to notice progress — not just problems.

It's not about bragging, it's about reinforcing the fact that you're capable, resilient, and worth rooting for.

3. Ways to Celebrate Without Feeling Cringe

- **Share the win**: "I just hit a milestone I never thought I could — and I'm proud of me."
- **Treat yourself**: Buy the coffee, wear the nice outfit, light the candle you've been "saving."
- **Document it**: Write it down, take the photo, make the memory.

4. Give Other People Permission to Shine

When you own your wins, you model to others that it's safe to do the same.

Your celebration might just give someone else the courage to say, "I'm proud of me too."

The point:

You've worked too hard to pretend your victories don't matter.

Celebrate them. Out loud. Often. And without apology.

Chapter 79: Becoming Unshakeable Without Becoming Unfeeling

Being strong doesn't mean turning into stone.

It means you can weather the storm without letting it harden you into someone you no longer recognise.

1. Understand What "Unshakeable" Really Means

It's not about never feeling hurt, it's about not letting hurt dictate your choices.

The most grounded people still feel everything... they just don't let every wave knock them off balance.

2. Drop the Armour, Keep the Spine

There's a difference between boundaries and emotional walls.

Boundaries say, *"This is what I will and won't allow."*

Walls say, *"No one gets in, ever."*

You need a spine, not a fortress.

3. Stay Human in the Process

- Let people see your humanity.
- Allow yourself to cry when something hurts.
- Laugh, even when things aren't perfect.

Strength without softness becomes isolation.

4. Balance Logic and Compassion

When someone wrongs you, the unshakeable version of you thinks:

- **Logic:** What's the truth here?
- **Compassion:** Can I respond without cruelty?

5. Remember: Stillness Is Power

You don't have to react to prove you're strong.

Sometimes the most powerful move is to stand calm while the chaos spins around you.

The point:

You can be unshakeable and still deeply feel.

The trick is letting your emotions inform you, not control you.

Chapter 80: How to Handle People Who Hate Your Boundaries

Some people will treat your boundaries like a locked door.

Instead of knocking, they'll jiggle the handle, shove it, or act offended that it's there at all.

Boundaries don't just protect you, they reveal who respects you.

1. Expect the Pushback

When you set a boundary, people who benefitted from your lack of one will feel it the most.

They may call you selfish, cold, or dramatic.

That's not a reflection of your boundary; it's a reflection of their entitlement.

2. Don't Over-Explain

You don't owe a 15-minute TED Talk every time you say *"no"*.

A simple, clear response works:

- "That doesn't work for me."
- "I'm not available for that."
- "No, thank you."

3. Hold the Line

Boundaries without follow-through are just suggestions.

If someone keeps stepping over your line, step back from them, even if they don't like it.

4. Neutral Is Your Superpower

Stay calm. Don't match their emotional outburst.

If you keep your voice steady and your body language relaxed, it shows your boundary is not up for negotiation.

5. Remember Your Why

Your boundary is there to protect your mental, emotional, or physical health, not to punish someone else.

When you remember that, it's easier to stand firm.

The point:

Boundaries aren't about controlling others; they're about controlling your access to peace.

And anyone who hates that was probably never rooting for your peace in the first place.

Chapter 81: When to Walk Away Before You Burn Out

Most of us are taught to "push through" when we're tired, stressed, or hanging on by a thread.

But pushing through is exactly how you end up resenting people, resenting commitments, and resenting yourself.

Walking away before burnout isn't weakness, it's strategy.

1. Spot the Early Warning Signs

Burnout doesn't happen overnight. Look for:

- Feeling heavy dread before even small interactions

- Snapping at people you normally like
- Physical symptoms (headaches, fatigue, stomach issues)
- Constantly daydreaming about disappearing

2. Give Yourself Permission to Quit

Quitting gets a bad rap. But there's a difference between quitting *on* yourself and quitting *for* yourself.

If something is draining you faster than it's filling you, stepping back is self-preservation.

3. Take a Temporary Step Back

You don't always have to cut ties forever.

Sometimes you just need:

- A weekend with your phone on Do Not Disturb
- A "hard pass" on optional events
- A few weeks where you don't answer every call

4. Reframe the Guilt

Guilt will try to convince you that walking away makes you a bad person.

Here's the truth: people who benefit from your over-giving will never be the ones to tell you to rest.

So you have to tell yourself.

5. Protect the Exit

Once you've decided to walk away, don't let guilt, pressure, or false promises pull you back in before you're ready.

Think of it like healing a wound, you wouldn't rip the stitches out early just because someone wanted you to.

The point:

You're allowed to leave situations, conversations, or commitments before they break you.

The people who love you will understand. The people who don't? They'll just prove you made the right choice.

Chapter 82: Building Emotional Muscle for the Long Game

Strong boundaries are like strong muscles, you don't build them once and expect them to last forever.

They need training, maintenance, and a plan for when life throws heavier weights your way.

1. Start Small and Stay Consistent

Emotional resilience isn't built through one dramatic "I'm done!" speech, it's built through a hundred tiny choices:

- Saying *no* without explaining
- Not responding to a guilt-tripping text
- Choosing your peace over winning the argument

2. Practice Recovery Time

Athletes rest between workouts so their muscles can rebuild stronger.

You need the same between emotional hits.

That means actually taking time to:

- Sleep properly
- Eat something that isn't stress fuel
- Do something that makes you laugh without thinking about "the situation"

3. Learn to Take the Hit Without Breaking

Resilience isn't about avoiding hurt, it's about not letting hurt own you.

When something knocks you sideways:

- Pause before reacting
- Name what you're feeling (instead of spiraling on what they did)

- Choose a response that won't leave you with a regret hangover

4. Train With Safe People First

Don't test your new boundaries on the most toxic person in your life.

Practice with people you trust, so it becomes second nature before you're in the high-stakes situations.

5. Remember the Long Game

Your emotional fitness isn't just about surviving *this* person or *this* season.

It's about building the strength to keep your peace no matter who comes into your life next.

Bottom line:

The more you train your boundaries, recovery time, and emotional balance, the less power anyone has, to knock you off your game.

Chapter 83: How to Spot Real Love and Real Friendship Early On

One of the biggest reasons we end up with toxic people is because we mistake *intensity* for *genuine care*.

The truth? The most dangerous relationships often start with fireworks… and the healthiest ones usually start with a steady glow.

1. Safe Feels Boring at First, And That's a Good Thing

If you're used to chaos, calm can feel like a lack of passion.

Real love and real friendship aren't adrenaline highs, they're the quiet safety of knowing you can just *be*.

2. Words and Actions Match

No disappearing acts. No "I'm just busy" for weeks on end.

Healthy people do what they say they'll do, even in the small stuff.

3. There's No Price Tag on Your Worth

You don't feel like you have to earn their kindness or affection.

Your value isn't tied to what you can do for them, they like you for *you*.

4. Disagreements Don't Become Punishments

They don't ice you out for days or hold grudges like a weapon.

Healthy connections solve problems instead of weaponising them.

5. You Can Show the Messy Parts Without Fear

You don't feel like you have to perform, mask, or sugarcoat every word.

With real people, you can be tired, silly, vulnerable, or even wrong — and the relationship doesn't crumble.

Bottom line:

Real love and friendship make your life bigger, not smaller. They give you more energy, not less. If you feel lighter, calmer, and more yourself around them, that's how you know you've found the real thing.

Chapter 84: The Self-Respect Checklist

Self-respect isn't a mysterious vibe you're either born with or not, it's a series of choices you make every day.

When you start checking these boxes consistently, your relationships change, your peace levels rise, and you stop being an easy target for manipulators.

1. You Keep Promises to Yourself

If you said you'd do it, you follow through, even if nobody else will know.

Every kept promise builds trust in yourself.

2. You Don't Explain 'No'

"No" is a complete sentence.

You don't owe anyone a detailed essay about your boundaries.

3. You Value Your Time as Much as Theirs

You stop waiting endlessly for people who can't be bothered to show up on time.

Your hours are just as important as anyone else's.

4. You Refuse to Compete for Basic Respect

You don't chase, bargain, or prove you deserve to be treated like a human being.

5. You Protect Your Energy Like It's Gold

You recognise when something drains you and limit your exposure to it — whether it's a person, place, or habit.

6. You Accept That Not Everyone Will Like You

And you stop auditioning for their approval.

Your peace matters more than being universally liked.

7. You Don't Let Loneliness Trick You Into Settling

You'd rather be alone than with someone who treats you badly.

Final note for Act 3:

Self-respect isn't about perfection, it's about alignment.

When your actions match your worth, you stop being walk-over material and start being the kind of person who can't be bought, broken, or bullied.

ACT 4 – The Quiet After the Storm

Loneliness, rebuilding, and loving the life you choose.

Chapter 85: Why Loneliness Isn't a Sign You've Done Something Wrong

When the noise stops, it can feel wrong.

After you cut ties with toxic friends, step away from draining family, or leave a relationship that was slowly killing your spirit, the silence hits. And for a while, it feels like you've made a huge mistake.

You haven't.

Loneliness Is Just the Space Between Versions of You

Think of it like moving out of an old, falling-apart house before your new one is ready.

There's an in-between stage where you're surrounded by boxes, the rooms echo, and it feels uncomfortable. But that's not failure, that's transition.

You Didn't Lose People, You Lost Distractions

When you clear out the wrong people, you also clear out the drama, the chaos, and the fake "connection" that came with them.

Loneliness is often just the absence of noise, not the absence of love.

It's the Proof Your Boundaries Worked

If you're lonely because you removed people who trampled your boundaries, congratulations, your boundaries did exactly what they were supposed to do.

The Temporary Discomfort Is Worth the Long-Term Gain

The right people don't rush in just because you made space.

That space needs to stay open long enough for the wrong ones to realise they can't come back and for the right ones to find you.

You're Not Broken, You're Healing

Loneliness after growth is not a punishment. It's your nervous system adjusting to peace, your heart learning that quiet doesn't mean danger, and your mind unlearning the idea that constant connection equals safety.

Bottom line:

You didn't do something wrong. You did something brave. And right now, the quiet is proof you're in the middle of building something better.

Chapter 86: How to Stop Romanticising the People You Walked Away From

Time is a skilled liar.

It blurs the bad parts, sharpens the good ones, and leaves you wondering if maybe you overreacted. Spoiler: you didn't.

Your Brain Has a Built-In Highlight Reel

When we miss someone, our mind loves to play the "best of" compilation. The laughs, the fun nights, the good conversations, all queued up on repeat. What it doesn't show you are the slow burns, the betrayals, and the exhaustion.

Memory Isn't an Accurate Historian, It's a Biased Screenwriter

Your brain will rewrite scenes to make them softer, cleaner, and more appealing than they actually were. But you can't heal if you keep editing the past to make it rewatchable.

Make the Bad Parts Impossible to Forget

Write down, yes, physically write, the reasons you walked away. The comments that cut deep. The actions that broke trust. The moments you felt small, unsafe, or unseen. Keep it where you can reach it when nostalgia tries to gaslight you.

Stop Treating "Missing Them" as a Sign You Were Wrong

Missing someone doesn't mean you made the wrong choice. It means you're human, you had a connection, and now there's a gap where that connection used to be. Gaps are uncomfortable. They are not evidence you should refill them with the same person.

Fall in Love With the Life You're Building

The fastest way to stop romanticising the past is to romanticise the present. Create moments in your current life that make you feel alive, peaceful, or inspired, so your mind has new highlight reels to play.

Bottom line:

Don't let nostalgia dress up your pain in a pretty costume. Remember it clearly, release it fully, and move forward without rewriting the truth.

Chapter 87: The Difference Between Being Alone and Being Lonely

Being alone is a physical state.

Loneliness is an emotional one.

You can be surrounded by people and still feel lonely, or you can be by yourself and feel completely content.

Alone Is Neutral, Loneliness Is a Feeling

"Alone" just means no one else is in the room. That's it. There's no value judgment, no automatic sadness attached. Loneliness, on the other hand, is the ache that comes when we feel unseen, unheard, or disconnected, even in company.

Loneliness Can Come From the Wrong People

The most painful kind of loneliness often happens in bad relationships. You're physically with someone, but emotionally starving. That's why leaving can feel both freeing and terrifying, you've removed the wrong person, but you still need to learn how to fill the space they left.

Being Alone Can Be a Power Move

When you choose to be alone, you're telling the world (and yourself) that your peace matters more than forced company. It's the difference between eating a meal you love solo and choking down something you hate just to avoid sitting at an empty table.

Turn Alone Time Into Connection With Yourself

Use it to ask, "What do I actually like?" and "What would I do right now if no one was judging me?" Read that weird book, dance in the kitchen, take a class just because it sounds fun. Make alone time a gift, not a punishment.

Bottom line:

Loneliness says, "I need connection." Being alone says, "I'm okay in my own company." Learn the difference, and you'll never confuse solitude with sadness again.

If you want, I can roll right into **Chapter 88: How to Fill Your Own Cup (Without Waiting for Someone Else to Pour)** so the tone stays connected.

Chapter 88: How to Fill Your Own Cup (Without Waiting for Someone Else to Pour)

If you're always waiting for someone else to notice you're running on empty, you'll stay thirsty forever.

The truth is, most people are too wrapped up in their own lives to see your cup, let alone fill it. That's not always selfishness, it's just reality.

Self-Filling Is Self-Respect

Filling your own cup isn't about rejecting help, it's about making sure your well-being isn't dependent on someone else's mood, availability, or approval. When you meet your own needs first, everything anyone else gives you is a bonus, not a lifeline.

Start Small and Daily

- **Rest** without guilt. You don't have to "earn" it.
- **Feed yourself well.** Nourishing food says, "I'm worth the effort."
- **Move your body** in a way that feels good, not punishing.
- **Do one thing you genuinely enjoy** every single day, even if it's just five minutes.

Stop Waiting for Permission

You don't need someone to tell you it's okay to take a break, buy the good coffee, or light the expensive candle. The longer you wait for external permission, the longer you put your happiness on layby.

Protect Your Pour

Your energy is like water, once it's gone, you can't pour it back. Say no to people, tasks, and dramas that constantly drain you without refilling anything in return.

Bottom line:

When you fill your own cup first, you stop living in scarcity and start living in overflow. From there, you can share, not because you have to, but because you actually want to.

Chapter 89: Relearning Fun Without an Audience

Somewhere along the way, we got tricked into thinking fun only "counts" if someone else sees it.

If it's not on Instagram, if nobody claps, if no one says "wow", did it even happen?

Yes. It did. And it matters even more.

Fun Without the Performance

When you strip the audience away, you strip away the pressure too. Suddenly, fun becomes about *you*, not about being interesting to anyone else. That's when you start rediscovering what actually lights you up.

Ways to Relearn Fun (No Witness Required)

- Dance in your kitchen like the tiles are your stage.
- Bake the cake *just* because it's Tuesday.
- Read a trashy novel under a blanket fort.
- Paint something ridiculous and hang it where only you see it.
- Go for a solo day trip with your favourite playlist.

Why This Matters

If your joy depends on someone else's reaction, you'll always be hustling for approval. Fun without an audience teaches you that you're allowed to feel joy for the sake of joy — no applause needed.

Bottom line:

The real magic is when you catch yourself smiling alone, and there's no one around to witness it — and you don't care. That's when you know the fun is finally yours again.

Chapter 90: Finding Peace in Your Own Company

For some people, being alone feels like a punishment. For others, it's the first deep breath they've taken in years. Learning to love your own company isn't about locking the door and becoming a hermit, it's about making peace with the person you spend the most time with… you.

Why It Feels Hard at First

When you're used to constant noise, family drama, toxic friendships, unhealthy relationships, silence can feel like a void. But the "quiet" is where you start hearing yourself again.

How to Build That Peace

- **Create rituals just for you**, morning coffee in your favourite mug, evening walks without your phone, a bath with the good candles (yes, the ones you were saving).
- **Make your home a comfort zone**, everything from your bed sheets to your playlist should say "safe."
- **Do solo check-ins**, ask yourself, "What do I need today?" and then actually give it to yourself.

The Shift

The more time you spend enjoying your own space and thoughts, the less desperate you feel to fill every gap with people who drain you. You stop accepting crumbs because you've built your own feast.

Bottom line:

When you can sit in a quiet room and feel content, you've found the kind of peace no one else can take away.

Chapter 91: The Joy of Saying "No Plans" and Meaning It

There's a certain magic in answering, "What are you doing this weekend?" with, "Absolutely nothing," and feeling zero guilt about it.

For too long, "no plans" was code for *please invite me so I don't look like a loser*. Now? It's a declaration of independence.

Why "No Plans" Is Powerful

- It means you're not filling your time with people or activities that drain you just to avoid being alone.
- It proves you've stopped measuring your worth by how busy your calendar looks.

- It gives you control over your time, and your energy.

How to Make the Most of a Plan-Free Day

- Sleep in without setting an alarm.
- Wander through a bookstore or market with no agenda.
- Re-watch your favourite show without someone asking, "Haven't you seen this already?"
- Have a snack picnic in bed, no fancy plates required.

The Rebellion in Rest

Toxic people thrive when you're exhausted, distracted, and too busy to notice their nonsense. A slow day with no commitments is a radical act of self-preservation.

Bottom line:

"No plans" isn't a lack of a life, it's the life you choose.

Chapter 92: Why Some Days Will Still Hurt (and That's Okay)

Healing isn't a straight line, it's a weird, twisty road with sudden potholes and the occasional emotional sinkhole.

You can be months into feeling stronger and more peaceful when out of nowhere, a memory, song, or random smell sucker-punches you back into the hurt. And that's… normal.

Why This Doesn't Mean You're Back at Square One

- Pain resurfacing is just your brain processing another layer, not undoing all your progress.

- The sting is often shorter and less intense than it used to be. That's growth, even if it doesn't feel like it.
- Your ability to comfort yourself now is miles ahead of where you started.

What to Do on the Hurt Days

- Let yourself cry without labelling it as weakness.
- Cancel plans if you need to, without apologising for it.
- Use your favourite grounding rituals, the tea, the walk, the playlist.
- Write down what triggered you and what you wish you could tell your past self in that moment.

The Secret Truth

Some things will never stop hurting completely. The goal isn't to erase the pain, it's to live a good, full, and joyful life *with* it.

Bottom line:

A hurt day is just a day, not your whole life. Let it pass, and you'll still be standing tomorrow, maybe even stronger.

Chapter 93: Making Your Home Your Safe Space

When the world feels overwhelming, your home should be the place that exhales for you.

Too many people live in spaces that hold stress instead of comfort, piles of clutter, reminders of people who hurt them, and constant visual noise. If your home doesn't feel like it's on your side, it's time to change that.

Start With What Doesn't Feel Good

- **Clear out triggers**, gifts from toxic exes, family drama heirlooms, or anything that makes you flinch when you see it.
- **Fix the small annoyances**, the squeaky door, the lightbulb you keep forgetting to change. Every little fix is a reminder that you can create order.

Add What Feels Safe and Soft

- Lighting that calms you, warm lamps instead of harsh overhead glare.
- A corner that's purely for comfort, whether it's a reading chair, a floor cushion, or your bed with ridiculously soft blankets.
- A scent you associate with calm, candles, essential oils, or fresh flowers.

Make It Yours Again

Rearrange furniture. Hang art that makes you smile. Play music that feels like *you*. The goal is for your home to reflect who you are now, not who you were when life was harder.

Bottom line:

Your home isn't just where you live, it's where you heal. Let it be a place that reminds you every day that you are safe, supported, and in control.

Chapter 94: The Beauty of Small, Consistent Routines

Grand transformations are built on boring, beautiful habits.

When you've lived in chaos, toxic relationships, unpredictable moods, or constant crises, routine can feel foreign, even uncomfortable. But small, steady actions are what quietly rewire your brain to expect safety instead of survival mode.

Start Tiny, Win Big

Don't overhaul your whole life at once. Choose one or two small things you can commit to daily:

- Making your bed.

- Drinking a full glass of water in the morning.
- Taking a 10-minute walk after lunch.

These aren't glamorous, but they build trust with yourself.

Why Small Wins Matter

Every time you follow through, your brain registers: *I can rely on me.* This is the opposite of the instability you may have experienced in relationships or family dynamics.

Anchor Points in Your Day

Having consistent moments you can look forward to, like a nightly cup of tea, journaling before bed, or stretching when you wake up, gives your mind and body signals that you're safe.

Bottom line:

Small routines aren't about control, they're about care. The more you show up for yourself in little ways, the easier it becomes to rebuild a life that feels calm, steady, and yours.

Chapter 95:
How to Date Yourself Without Feeling Silly

If you're waiting for someone else to make you feel special, you'll always be at their mercy. Dating yourself means you stop putting your joy on layaway until "the right person" shows up.

The Mindset Shift

It's not "sad" to take yourself out, it's self-respect. You're showing yourself the same energy you'd happily pour into someone else, but without the risk of them texting you "U up?" six months later.

Ideas to Get You Started

- **Café Date** – Take a book or journal, order your favourite drink, and people-watch like it's your full-time job.
- **Gallery Stroll** – Wander through art exhibits and pretend you're a mysterious collector.
- **Solo Movie Night** – No sharing popcorn, no commentary unless it's from you.
- **Nature Walk** – Talk to the ducks. They're better listeners than most exes.

Own the Awkwardness

The first few times might feel weird, especially if you've always had someone by your side. But the more you do it, the more you realise that you're *good company*.

Bottom line:

Date yourself the way you wish someone else would, not to fill a void, but to prove to yourself that you were never incomplete in the first place.

Chapter 96: Finding New Hobbies Without the Friend Drama

If your hobbies used to come with a side of gossip, competition, or "accidentally" not inviting you to the next meet-up, it's time to reclaim your interests, minus the chaos.

Why This Matters

Toxic people have a way of making you associate your hobbies with tension. They turn something fun into another arena for judgment. The trick is to detach the activity from the people who ruined it.

Steps to Start Fresh

1. **Pick Something That's Yours**, choose a hobby you've never shared with the old crowd. New activity = no old baggage.

2. **Go Solo First**, Learn the ropes on your own before deciding whether you want to join a group or class.
3. **Avoid Drama Hotspots**, If a space is known for cliques or competitive energy, skip it.
4. **Set Social Boundaries Early**, If you join a class or club, decide upfront how much personal info you'll share.

Hobby Inspiration

- Indoor climbing, paddleboarding, or pottery
- Baking something no one else gets to taste but you
- Taking online classes in a skill, you've always wanted
- Joining a virtual community that values kindness over competition

Bottom line:

Hobbies are supposed to feed your soul, not drain it. The right activity won't just entertain you; it will rebuild your sense of self without the static of other people's baggage.

Chapter 97: How to Make Peace with "It Ended"

Endings are uncomfortable. They feel like unfinished sentences, like you're still waiting for the "but" or "unless" that will make it all okay. But sometimes the most healing thing you can do is stop waiting for the sequel that will never be written.

Why This Hurts So Much

Your brain craves closure. It wants the missing puzzle piece, the apology, the "now it makes sense."

But closure isn't always delivered in a neat box. Sometimes it's something you have to give yourself.

Steps Toward Peace

1. **Acknowledge What Was Real** – It happened. The good parts and the bad parts both existed. You can hold them without rewriting the past.
2. **Accept the Lack of Answers** – They may never explain. They may never see your side. You can still move forward.
3. **Remove the 'What Ifs'** – Keep them from circling by replacing them with "Even if."
    - "*Even if they come back, I won't return to the same dynamic.*"
4. **Let the Grief Move** – Write it out, talk it out, or walk it out. Stuck grief keeps you stuck in the ending.
5. **Redefine the Story** – See it as a chapter in *your* life, not the whole book.

A Gentle Reminder

Sometimes we think peace will come the moment they give us the explanation, apology, or confession we're owed. The truth? Peace comes when we decide their silence doesn't control our story anymore.

If you can make peace with an ending, you give yourself permission to write a better beginning.

Chapter 98: Choosing the Right People to Let Back In

When you've finally found peace, the last thing you want is to hand it over to someone who once broke it. But life has a funny way of circling people back to you, sometimes reformed, sometimes rehearsed.

The Gatekeeper Mindset

Think of yourself as the gatekeeper to your life. Not everyone who knocks gets a key. Not everyone who once had one should get a duplicate.

Questions to Ask Before You Unlock the Door

1. **Have They Changed, or Just Circumvented Consequences?**
   - Look for actions, not apologies. A changed person doesn't just talk about growth; they *show* it.
2. **Can You Trust Them Without Monitoring Them?**
   - If you have to keep tabs, you're not letting them back in — you're letting them back *on probation*.
3. **Do They Respect the New Boundaries?**
   - If they test your limits right away, they're showing you they haven't earned the space.
4. **Does Their Presence Add More Peace Than Stress?**
   - Check your gut. Peace feels light, tension feels heavy.
5. **Are You Letting Them In Out of Love or Loneliness?**
   - Reconnection based on loneliness almost always reopens old wounds.

Signs They're Safe to Let Back In

- They acknowledge the past without defensiveness.
- They've stopped the behaviours that caused harm.
- They respect your independence and choices.
- They bring genuine joy and not conditional kindness.

Final Thought

Forgiveness is a gift you give yourself. Access is a privilege they have to earn.

You can love someone from a distance, and sometimes that distance is the healthiest version of the relationship you'll ever have.

Chapter 99: The Science of Building New Neural Pathways for Joy

Healing isn't just emotional, it's neurological. Every time you repeat a thought or behaviour, your brain strengthens that pathway. If you've spent years stuck in people-pleasing, toxic relationship patterns, or self-doubt, your brain has built *superhighways* for stress and self-sabotage. The good news? You can rewire them.

Neuroplasticity: Your Brain's Superpower

Neuroplasticity is your brain's ability to form new connections and ditch the old ones. Think of it like renovating a house, you can pull out the ugly old carpet of toxic patterns and lay down a new floor of joy, self-respect, and healthy habits.

How to Build Joy Pathways

1. **Small, Repeated Acts of Happiness**
    - Joy doesn't have to be fireworks. It can be morning coffee in your favourite mug, stepping outside for five minutes of sun, or playing a song that makes you move.
    - Repeat these small acts daily. Your brain starts linking them with safety and calm.
2. **Swap "Why Me?" for "What's Next?"**
    - Language shapes your brain's wiring. Asking "What's next?" puts you in solution mode instead of victim mode.
3. **Celebrate Micro-Wins**
    - Your brain thrives on reward. Every time you acknowledge progress — no matter how tiny — you're reinforcing the new neural pathway.
4. **Limit Time on Old Pathways**
    - Rumination is like watering weeds. The less time you give to

toxic thoughts, the faster they fade.
5. **Anchor Joy to Rituals**
    - Tie joy to things you already do. For example, every time you brush your teeth, think of one thing you're grateful for.

The 90-Second Rule

When you feel a negative emotion, your brain only needs 90 seconds to process the chemical surge, unless *you* keep feeding it with thoughts. Learn to let that first wave pass before deciding how to react.

Final Thought

You're not stuck with the wiring you have now. You can build a brain that's more in love with peace than with drama, more wired for joy than for pain.

Every small, intentional act is a brick in the road to the life you want. Keep laying them, one joyful step at a time.

Chapter 100: When Loneliness Turns into Freedom

At first, loneliness feels like a void, the silence after years of constant noise. You notice the empty space on the couch, the quiet mornings, the absence of "just checking in" texts that were actually control disguised as care.

And in the early days, that quiet can feel heavy. You might even wonder if you've made a mistake.

But something shifts. One day, you realise the silence isn't empty anymore, it's spacious. It's yours.

The Freedom in the Space

1. **No More Permission Slips**

- You don't have to check in with anyone before making plans, buying something, or even just… resting.
2. **Energy on Your Terms**
    - You decide where your time and emotional energy go. No more draining conversations or endless explanations.
3. **Room to Grow**
    - The absence of toxic voices leaves space for your own voice to get louder, clearer, and kinder.
4. **The End of Walking on Eggshells**
    - Freedom feels like wearing your favourite hoodie, you're just comfortable being yourself.

Signs You've Crossed the Line from Lonely to Free

- You start enjoying your own company more than forced socialising.
- You choose who gets access to you instead of letting everyone in by default.
- You feel lighter, even on days when you're physically alone.

- You laugh, really laugh, and no one has to be there to cause it.

A Gentle Reminder

Freedom isn't about never letting anyone close again. It's about knowing you can be whole without them. That your life doesn't collapse if someone walks away.

Because the moment you stop fearing solitude, you become untouchable.

Chapter 101:
The First Laugh After the Storm

It happens when you least expect it.

Maybe it's during a silly meme scroll at midnight, or while watching a bad reality show where someone dramatically throws wine for no reason.

At first, the laugh surprises you. It's been so long since it felt this easy, this unforced. It escapes before you can stop it, bubbling up like sunlight after weeks of rain.

Why This Laugh Matters

This isn't just a moment of amusement, it's proof.

Proof that your joy didn't die with that relationship, that friendship, or that season of life.

It's been hiding, waiting for its cue to step back into the spotlight.

The Science Bit

Laughter physically shifts your body out of stress mode. Endorphins kick in. Your nervous system softens. For a second, you're not thinking about what was lost, you're living in what's here.

The Ripple Effect

That one laugh opens the door to more:

- The giggle you can't suppress when your pet does something ridiculous.

- The snort-laugh over an inside joke you have with yourself.
- The full, unrestrained belly laugh that makes your cheeks hurt.

A Small Promise to Yourself

Don't feel guilty when you laugh too soon, or not soon enough. Joy isn't a betrayal of what you've been through, it's the rebellion that keeps you alive.

Chapter 102: Why "Better Alone" Can Be Better Forever

The world loves to romanticise "finding your person" as the ultimate life achievement. Movies end with weddings, songs obsess over soulmates, and Aunt Karen keeps asking when you're going to "settle down."

But here's the quiet truth no one puts on greeting cards:

Sometimes the best relationship you'll ever have is with yourself.

The Freedom in Choosing You

When you're alone, every choice is yours.

- You decorate your space exactly how you want, even if it's fairy lights in the bathroom and a hot pink kettle.
- You eat breakfast for dinner without explaining it to anyone.
- You spend weekends however you like, without compromise.

There's no emotional tax to pay for someone else's mood, no silent resentment building over unspoken expectations.

The Myth of "Incomplete"

Society sells the idea that single = lonely, but that's a marketing ploy for dating apps and wedding industries.

Wholeness isn't something you gain through another person, it's something you already have, but maybe forgot to notice.

When Alone Feels Lighter

Being alone can mean:

- **No more pretending** you're okay with behaviours that hurt you.
- **No more shrinking** yourself to fit someone else's comfort zone.
- **No more fighting** for crumbs of attention when you deserve the feast.

Better Alone ≠ Forever Alone

This isn't a vow to never let love in. It's a refusal to invite anything in that isn't real love. The right people will add to your life, not drain it. Until then, your own company is not a waiting room. It's the main event.

Chapter 103: How to Spot When You're Ready to Connect Again

After a season of protecting your peace like it's the crown jewels, the thought of letting new people in can feel... risky.

Opening your heart (or even your calendar) to others again isn't about forcing yourself to "be social." It's about recognising when the foundations you've built are strong enough to handle new connections without shaking apart.

Signs You Might Be Ready

1. You're Not Looking for a Lifeline

You want connection because you're curious and open, not because you're desperate to be "saved" from loneliness.

2. You Can Say No Without Fear

Boundaries feel like normal conversation, not a high-stakes battle.

3. You're Not Haunted by the Past

The people who hurt you no longer take up mental real estate; they're just old characters from a story you've finished reading.

4. You Feel Excited, Not Anxious

The idea of meeting someone new sparks interest instead of dread.

5. You Trust Yourself to Walk Away

You know you can leave any dynamic that stops feeling right, without guilt or explanation.

Connection as a Choice, Not a Need

When you're ready, you don't chase connection. You allow it. You meet people where they are, without trying to turn them into something they're not. You notice red flags without writing love stories around them.

The New Rule

You don't have to open every door that knocks.

You choose carefully, because you've worked too hard to let chaos rent space in your life again.

Chapter 104: The New Life You Build Is the Real Revenge

They say the best revenge is living well, but honestly? It's living so well you forget there was ever anything to avenge.

When you've been through heartbreak, betrayal, or toxic family dynamics, it's tempting to want them to *see* you thriving. You imagine posting that perfect photo, delivering that killer speech, or walking past them looking like you invented self-respect.

But here's the truth: the real power move is when you stop caring if they're watching.

The Shift

Revenge is fuelled by them.

Rebuilding is fuelled by you.

When your focus moves from proving them wrong to proving yourself right, you stop running your life on spite and start running it on joy, purpose, and peace.

What This Looks Like

- Your mornings start with gratitude instead of anxiety.
- Your relationships feel like a safe home, not a battlefield.
- You make choices based on what feels good for *you*, not what will shock *them*.
- You smile without thinking about who's noticing.

The Quiet Win

The real revenge isn't loud. It's the day you wake up and realise you've built a life so rich, so safe, and so yours… that their opinions no longer even register.

Because the final chapter of your story isn't about them.

It's about the woman who refused to stay broken, even when the world expected her to.

About the Author

Holly Symons writes with one mission in mind: to help women protect their peace, spot red flags before they turn into disasters, and build stronger, healthier connections. With a mix of sharp insight and relatable humour, she turns complicated relationship patterns into clear, actionable advice anyone can use.

Her work especially resonates with neurodivergent women, who often find themselves over-giving, over-explaining, or attracting the wrong people. Holly breaks down these patterns into simple, practical steps that make it easier to set boundaries and choose relationships that truly feel safe and supportive.

Whether it's navigating fake friends, difficult family members, or lonely seasons in life, Holly's words are designed to empower women to choose themselves first, always, and to walk away knowing they deserve more, not less

BEFORE YOU CLOSE THIS BOOK...

If anything you've read here brought up more than you expected, please remember this - you don't have to carry it alone.

Sometimes, when we start recognising crumbs for what they are, we also remember the moments we went hungry for love, respect, or kindness. That can feel heavy. If you're feeling upset, anxious, or hopeless right now, it's okay to reach out for a hand.

Here are some places to start:

AUSTRALIA – Lifeline: Call 13 11 14 or text 0477 13 11 14

USA & CANADA – 988 Suicide & Crisis Lifeline: Call or text 988

UK & IRELAND – Samaritans: Call 116 123 (freephone)

Your story isn't over. You are not alone. And just in case no one's told you today - you deserve more than crumbs. Always.

www.ingramcontent.com/pod-product-compliance
Lightning Source LLC
Chambersburg PA
CBHW071145070526
44584CB00019B/2660